GRAND
CANYON
GHOST
STORIES

GRAND
CANYON
GHOST
STORIES

DEBE BRANNING

RIVERBEND
PUBLISHING

To all of my friends who have hiked with me down into the depths of the Grand Canyon and experienced its inner beauty and waterfalls, have walked with me along the scenic pathways of the Rim Trail, and have come to appreciate this natural wonder as more than just a "Golly Gully."

Grand Canyon Ghost Stories
© 2012 Debe Branning

ISBN 13: 978-1-60639-032-0

Cover design by Sarah Cauble, sarahcauble.com

Front cover photo: Desert View Watchtower in Grand Canyon National Park.

Text design by Barbara Fifer

Riverbend Publishing
P.O. Box 5833
Helena, MT 59604
1-866-787-2363
www.riverbendpublishing.com

CONTENTS

I stood viewing the Grand Canyon at the South Rim and wondered how the early tourists felt seeing this natural wonder for the first time. They traveled great distances by horse-drawn wagons or coaches, trains or, later, automobiles with great anticipation to gaze out at the landmark they had only read about. Back then there were no guard rails, stone walls or viewing restrictions. I have seen vintage photographs of women in long dresses and boots standing on rocks near the very edge of the rim. There are photos of formally dressed men and women astride mules on primitive trails ready for the adventure ride of a lifetime. What fabulous stories they must have told their children and grandchildren!

And that is how legends and ghost stories begin. Some of these tales have been past down through decades. They describe residual haunts that seem to happen over and over again. New mysteries and ghosts of the Grand Canyon surface from time to time as people become more aware of their senses and the paranormal world. *Grand Canyon Ghost Stories* is a collection of legends and tales told by Native Americans, Grand Canyon National Park employees, guests, and residents of Grand Canyon Village.

The best part of researching this book was talking to all of the people who have had their own personal experiences with the ghosts or legends of the Grand Canyon. It gave me a whole new perspective and appreciation for the area. Grand Canyon pioneers turned a large gaping hole in the ground into one of the world's most beloved treasures and tourist attractions. It is no wonder why ghosts of these brave souls continue to make the Grand Canyon their ultimate ghostly vacation destination.

I have hiked down into the depths of the canyon and felt the eerie spirits of the Native Americans and early explorers. It changes you for the rest of your lifetime. Strolling through the historic buildings along the rim allows you to walk in the footsteps of the pioneers who built the hotels, lookout points, and trails. Whether you are an avid hiker, someone who comes to relax and enjoy the view or a paranormal investigator hot on the trail after a ghost, I believe you will thoroughly enjoy these tales.

Remember that just because you can't see a ghost with your eyes does not mean there is no ghost present! Sometimes you can only hear a ghost or simply have a feeling of an unseen presence in the room with you. Sometimes a ghost will move things, flick lights on and off, or hide things from you. Some ghost stories are merely legends passed down through the centuries. Gather around the campfire, roast some marshmallows, and let your imagination run with the spirits and tales of the Grand Canyon's ghosts! Nighty-night!

A HISTORIAN'S SUPERNATURAL EXPERIENCE IN THE GRAND CANYON

My only supernatural experience at the canyon is when I hiked the old Hopi Salt Trail once, over by the Little Colorado River. That was the route where the Hopis, having left the third world at the Sipapuni (six miles upstream from the Colorado River), hiked into the fourth world, where they live today.

It was a lingering, overall feeling that I did not belong there, and at one point a peregrine falcon dive-bombed me and passed about three feet from my head at a hundred and fifty miles per hour. I made a conscious decision then never to go back!

Others I have talked to have had similar experiences, but these aren't really ghost stories. The Hopis believe it with all their hearts—it is part of their religion, so to speak.

I am typically skeptical of supernatural events, but what happened and what I felt were real.

—Michael F. Anderson, Ph.D.,
former teacher and guide for
the Grand Canyon Field Institute,
retired National Park Service trails archeologist
at Grand Canyon, and author of
three canyon histories

SPIRITS OF THE CAMERON TRADING POST

L ocated fifty miles north of Flagstaff on US Route 89, Cameron Trading Post sits high on a cliff above the Little Colorado River—a tributary to the mighty Colorado River that flows through the Grand Canyon.

In 1911, a swaybacked, one-lane suspension bridge was constructed over the Little Colorado River as the first route over the gorge. Two brothers, Hubert and C.D. Richardson, established the Cameron Trading Post in 1916. The post was named after Ralph Cameron, Arizona's last territorial delegate before statehood in 1912, and was located on a dirt road a few yards from the river. The nearby suspension bridge provided convenient access for the Indian neighboring tribes. Navajos and Hopis visited first, coming to barter and trade their wool, blankets, and livestock for dry goods.

9

Navajo stone masons built the post's stout buildings. The original structure still stands near the river, exhibiting several additions and modifications created through the years. The trading post now houses a curio and gift shop, and a beautifully restored dining room. The large dining facility offers a wall of large windows overlooking the Little Colorado River.

A trip to the trading post back in the early 1900s could take a few days of travel by horse-drawn wagon. Visitors were treated like family—fed and housed by trading staff during their stay.

In the early 1900s, the Richardson brothers operated several trading posts near the Grand Canyon area, including Cameron, Blue Canyon, Red Lake, Shonto, and Inscription House. They took time to learn local dialects and customs, and were trusted by the local Native American people in matters involving the American legal and social systems. The Navajo and Hopi told them stories, and they responded by translating these tales to travelers visiting the post.

Eventually, the roads improved and a new interest in tourism began to grow. The Cameron Trading Post's location, convenient to the Grand Canyon and other fascinating areas, made it a popular stop with early travelers.

In 1928, the brothers added a three-story building that served as a small hotel and Hubert Richardson's home. This sandstone structure is now a gallery that offers fine contemporary and antique Native American art.

Art gallery employees often feel they are not alone when working in what was once the old hotel's lobby. At one time there were four hotel rooms upstairs, available on any given night for weary travelers making their way though canyon lands, but now the upstairs is an art gallery. Employees often hear the sound of a man's heavy footsteps walking through the gallery rooms during business hours. Thinking it may be a customer, a staff member dashes upstairs to make a sale—only to find the gallery empty. Maybe the energy comes from the antique relics that adorn the building, or maybe it is from the dinosaur tracks embedded into the sandstone rocks inlaid upon the walls.

The employees sense their work is monitored by an unseen presence. They feel the ghost could be Hubert Richardson, who resided in the former hotel and was always the dominant figure in operating the hotel and post. He was a perfectionist and had to be sure the operation was running smoothly. Overhead lights in the lobby flicker on and off on their own accord—especially on days when things just aren't going according to plan.

"It is like the ghost is making sure things are done the proper way," the young clerk told us, "and the lights will keep turning back on until we have correctly closed down the shop and the cash registers balance for the day."

Cameron's secret garden spot is tucked away in a hidden courtyard behind the art gallery. Richardson's wife, Mabel, created the captivating courtyard gardens and added meandering sandstone pathways and a large fountain in the 1930s. The walkway is lined with beautiful roses and colorful blooms of many plants and trees. It's not surprising that the garden helped give the post an early nickname, "The Oasis." You can still relax near the tranquil fountain, enjoy the view, and perhaps hear voices of the past.

Employees say Hubert Richardson's spirit energy is felt everywhere on the property. Old photographs of Richardson and the Cameron Trading Post line the walls. His collections of Native American relics are showcased in frame-and-glass displays.

Today the Cameron Trading Post is owned by the people who work there. Many of them have had family roots in the area for generations. The restaurant, open for breakfast, lunch and dinner, serves Mexican and Navajo food, and is famous for its Navajo Taco.

The wait staff was happy to show us around the Cameron Restaurant Dining Room, where paranormal activity has been known to occur.

"Ghosts or what we call 'shadow people' (shadowy forms of humans) have been seen walking in the dining room," one waitress told us. "It usually happens near our nine P.M. closing time."

She led us to a back dining room that was constructed in recent years as an addition to the original building.

"There used to be an alleyway between the restaurant and an old motel in this spot. They tore down the motel and built on the annex to the restaurant and trading post," she explained. "Now employees and guests see what looks like 'transparent people' walking through where the former passageway was. Some guests say they are poked or pushed aside by the large strong hands of an unseen man while being seated at a table. We have witnessed a ghost of an elderly man from the early 1900s era sitting in a chair smoking a pipe or a cigar near the doorway many times."

A weathered upright piano sits along the same wall.

"We have heard the piano playing a lively old dance tune on several evenings." She recalled, "When we come into the room to catch the piano player, the room is always vacant. Again...this all happens at closing time."

"Who do you think the ghosts are?" we asked.

"I think it could be the Richardsons...or maybe Edward. Edward was a dedicated former employee at the post and rarely missed a day of work. He never left his assigned work-day tasks unfinished. He has passed away now, but he could still be making sure everything is in order," she smiled.

Jimmy, who has worked at Cameron Trading Post for over twenty-six years, told us he heard there is a ghost of a little pioneer girl who has been seen darting back and forth in front of the large stone fireplace in the dining room. Nobody knows her identity. It is feared she may have drowned in the Little Colorado River during one of the floods at Tanner Crossing along the Mormon Trail. Tanner Crossing is only a quarter mile from the trading post.

"The spirit of the Cameron Trading Post comes around at the close of the day," Jimmy confirmed the others' reports. "Usually when something is just not right—sometimes, we are not even aware of it—but it will always let us know."

Jimmy led us into the sales rooms at the front of the building and pointed up to the ceiling.

"See those lights?" he asked, waving his hand. "They are on a lighting track that is supposed to be even throughout the trading post. We were doing some remodeling a couple of years ago and hired an electrician to lay out the new lighting tracks. I watched him work and told him everything was crooked and he needed to re-measure to make the track square with the building. The electrician became angry and left for the day."

He led us over to a window and pointed over to the art gallery.

"I had to go over to the gallery and close it up for the evening," he explained. "I shut off the lights, locked the door, and walked back over here to the post so I could assess the electrician's work. I looked over my shoulder and the light was back on in the gallery. I walked back over and flipped the switch off once more. I then headed back to the post to lock up for the night. I set the alarm, turned off the lights, and locked the door. Looking to my left, I saw that the lights in the gallery had been turned on once again."

Jimmy shrugged his shoulders.

"Thinking I was going crazy, I hurried to the gallery and shut the lights off a third time. I was living across the highway back then, so I walked home and got ready for bed. Just as I lay down to sleep, I looked out the window and saw the gallery light glowing in the dark. I threw my clothes on, slipped into my shoes, and stomped back to the gallery—this time I was just a little annoyed."

"Do you know how expensive it is to keep the electricity on?" He barked at the unseen sentinel of the post.

Jimmy went back home but could not sleep well that night. He knew the lighting job had to be done right or his boss would blame him! Early the next morning, he walked back over to the post and waited for the electrician's return. But, instead of completing the job, the workman simply gathered the rest of his tools and took off. Jimmy completed the lighting installation himself.

"The light coming on and off in the gallery has become a signal to us that something is out of balance on the property," Jimmy explained. "Sometimes the light will alert us that the cash registers are out of balance, the floors are not swept, or the trash was not taken outside, or other closing duties were not completed correctly. Once the tasks have been competed the lights cease to flicker."

"So, in a sense, you have a double alarm system," I said, smiling. "One electronically scrutinized and one ancestrally monitored."

"Yes!" Jimmy nodded, "indeed we do!"

Be sure to make the Cameron Trading Post one of your haunts when going to and from the Grand Canyon. The new Cameron Trading Post Lodge offers modern accommodations sixty minutes way from Grand Canyon. They'll "leave the light on for you"...and off...and on.

Cameron Trading Post
466 Hwy 89
Cameron, AZ 86020
Gift Shop & Admin: 1-800-338-7385 or 1-928-679-2231

ETERNAL
CHILDREN AT
THE EDGE

Grand Canyon National Park boasts designated spectacular viewing points strung out along the canyon's South Rim. These lookout points offer visitors marvelous views of the canyon from every possible direction. Little did the construction teams know that some of the inspiration points would be the sites of suicides, murder, or careless accidents! The drop is steep and almost always fatal. Some viewing locations are very secluded. A murder could easily go undiscovered for years. There have been several accidental falls by visitors who slipped past the guard rails and lost their footing on the rocky terrain. Some tourists have witnessed a ghost or two near Grand Canyon overlooks, and believe they have returned to replay their last moments before their fatal descents.

Witnesses say they have seen a black misty figure near the railings at Maricopa Point at sundown. A man working for the Civilian Conservation Corps fell over the edge as he installed railings during the 1930s. A fairly loud scraping sound is heard as this figure goes through the motions of shoveling the hard ground.

The Little Colorado River lookout is one of the first stops visitors make if they are entering the Grand Canyon from its Eastern Gateway, or one of their last pit stops when leaving. Native American arts and craft workers arrive at sunrise each day to sell their wares from tables protected by covered stalls. This tradition has been in full swing since travelers began driving along the desolate highway on the way to the Grand Canyon. In earlier days, the Navajo pottery, leather goods and jewelry were placed on blankets along the ground near the lookout point.

The overlook has rest areas with ramadas, fireplaces, and picnic tables to provide a good resting point for the weary sightseer. Metal hand rails provide safety as the modern walkway takes visitors right up to the jagged canyon's edge. The picnic ground is a short walk from the overlook and offers a fine view of the deep, narrow gorge of the Little Colorado River. The finely layered upper limestone cliffs contrast with massive sandstone blocks below, evidence of a shallow sea 250 million years ago.

In June 1958, the vacationing Qualls family from Texas stopped here to take a look and photograph the Little Colorado River on their way to the southern rim of the Grand Canyon. James Lloyd Qualls, age five, and his younger brother, Harold Frank Qualls, fifteen months old, were among the family party. Their father, Frank Qualls, had parked the family sedan in a primitive parking lot near the lookout point on the rim just eight miles west of Cameron. Their father had left the transmission in gear—in the highest gear of over-drive, which provided the least resistance if the sedan began rolling. Qualls had not bothered to set the parking brake. Since the adults and older children were going to be out of the car only for a few minutes to capture a couple of scenic photos on their Kodak camera, they left the two younger boys unattended in the vehicle

The adults were merely 200 feet away from their car as they admired the fabulous view in the distance. They sent their ten-year-old relative, Kenneth Dull, back to the sedan to retrieve another camera stored in the glove compartment. Kenneth later said the vehicle started to roll as soon as he reached out to touch the door handle. Frightened, he jumped back away from the moving car. In those days, the parking area was slightly sloped, and there were no guard rails to protect visitors. After rolling merely 25 feet, the runaway car plummeted over the rim 1000 feet into the gorge. It bounced off the rocky terrain, and burst into flames. The two boys inside were killed.

Jennifer, one of the talented jewelry designers at the viewing point, told an interesting story about a gentleman who may have encountered the Quall children on his own Grand Canyon adventure in the summer of 2009. The traveler pulled into the parking lot with his camper truck just as the sun was setting. He had stopped at the craft area earlier that day and found a piece of work that really caught his eye. He hesitated about buying the item, but could not get its beauty and design out of his mind. He decided to return to the lookout point to make his purchase. To his dismay, the artist had already packed up and gone home for the day. The traveler was so disappointed. He really wanted that piece of jewelry. He knew he would never find another item quite like it. Jennifer, who was packing up her wares, suggested he could camp in the parking lot since that particular jeweler arrived daily at sunrise. This way, the visitor could make his purchase and still get an early start on his travels.

He agreed to the splendid idea and parked his truck in the visitor parking lot near the lookout point. The rest of the craft makers soon left. The tourist made himself a sandwich and prepared to bed down in the back of his camper. At about 1:00 A.M. he woke up, startled to hear the sound of children playing near his vehicle. He had believed he was the only person camping in the parking lot. He peeked out through the camper's curtains and thought he saw two small children playing just outside. Fearing he was hallucinating, he sat back down and poured himself a cold glass of water. A few minutes later he heard children giggling and laughing in the still air. He forced himself to take another look into the darkness. There were no lights in the parking lot to aid his eyesight, only the dim glow of a full moon.

Now he could plainly see the two children at play. They were boys, and they seemed to be getting closer to the rim of the gorge. Having grandchildren of his own, the man was terrified. He grabbed his flashlight and stepped outside, wondering if another family had camped nearby and lost sight of their children. He could not understand why anyone would let their offspring play alone in the dark at such a dangerous location. He stood near his camper and looked around, seeing that his was indeed the only vehicle in the parking lot. He continued to keep an eye on the frolicking children dressed in checkered buttoned-up shirts, tan shorts, and sneakers. The two of them seemed to be enjoying each other's company—but also seemed to be moving closer and closer to the edge.

"I have to get them away from the edge," the visitor thought, "before one of them gets hurt."

He slowly walked toward the pair, trying not to startle them. The closer he approached, the closer they appeared to be to the canyon rim. Suddenly, holding hands, the children disappeared from view as though they had fallen over the rocky edge. Do the unfortunate souls of the Qualls children still visit the world they once knew?

Another craftsman said he has also heard the voices of the lost children. There have been times when, just after sundown, he was the last artist to pack up for the day. The winds were calm but he could hear children crying near the rim of the gorge. He said nobody likes to be in the Little Colorado lookout area after dark. The still air is often interrupted by a strong wind, and you feel as though you are being watched. This sudden change is said to indicate the presence of "skin walkers" at the isolated lookout. Dark shadows, or "shape shifters," have been seen darting about the plateau. In some Native American legends, a person with the supernatural ability to turn into any animal he or she desires is a skin walker. They are usually wearing the pelt of the animal they are about to transform to. They are sometimes seen as a coyote, wolf, owl, fox, or crow. A shape shifter is a being who has the ability to alter its physical appearances—perhaps because of a curse or spell.

When making your stop at the Little Colorado Lookout point, be sure to set the parking brake, and don't be lured too close to the edge by unattended mischievous children. They could be trying to take you along for the ride of your life.

DESERT VIEW WATCHTOWER'S OBSESSIVE PRESENCE

The Harvey Company needed a gift shop and rest area on the eastern rim drive for Grand Canyon sightseers coming from or heading to the Cameron Trading Post about twenty-five miles farther east.

The Indian Watchtower at Desert View, a seventy-foot stone building, was created for this purpose on the South Rim. Four stories tall, it was completed in 1932. Its designer, architect Mary Colter, also created several other buildings in the Grand Canyon area. The Watchtower is often mistaken for an ancient ruin, and that is exactly the way Colter wanted it to appear. Her objective was to create a feeling of mystery.

From a distance, the building's silhouette looks like the Anasazi watchtower it was meant to mimic. But the structure is taller than any known Indian tower and has a much greater diameter. Its reddish sandstone is shaped into one large circle at the north, and a small circle at the south, with gently arched forms connecting the two.

During the Watchtower's construction, it is said that Colter was obsessed with the site, visiting at all hours of the day and night to be sure that shadows fell just right along the stone walls. Colter personally selected the stones used on the Watchtower and they were strategically placed into her design. Workmen were forced to tear down sections of the building if she wasn't completely satisfied. She added a strangely shaped rock that she called the Balolookong after the mythical snake in the Hopi culture, and placed other intriguingly-shaped rocks in various locations.

The tower's interior was decorated with Indian cave and wall drawings. Colter hired a young Hopi artist named Fred Kabotie to paint the murals in the Hopi Room. He created artwork on the interior walls that traced Hopi mythology. The other paintings were copies of designs of ancient New Mexico rock art.

The ground floor of the Watchtower was designed as a large round observation room with spectacular views of the Grand Canyon. The circular structure with a fireplace resembled a kiva, or room used for Native American spiritual ceremonies. It was to be used as a gift shop and museum of Hopi culture and symbolism. It is still operating as the Watchtower gift shop.

The Watchtower was celebrated with a dedication ceremony on May 13, 1933. The original opening day events included a traditional Hopi kiva blessing ceremony. A chant led by the Keeper of the Kiva thanked the spirits for their presence.

The first floor of the tower displays an open Hopi Snake altar while the upper floors offer an observation deck where visitors can view eastern portions of the Grand Canyon. The trapezoidal plate glass windows add vivid colors to the views of the Grand Canyon landscape. Desert View Watchtower was named as a U.S. National Historic Landmark on May 28, 1987.

A climb to the top of the tower is breathtaking, and the scenery from the viewing areas is spectacular. On a clear day one can see as far east as the Painted Desert and the Colorado River winding through Marble Gorge. The ceiling was constructed of logs salvaged from the old Grand View Hotel near the canyon rim. On your way to each floor be sure to keep your senses sharp for a bit of spectral activity known to sweep through the tower in the form of a cold breeze whipping up the spiral staircase.

Shop clerks have reported strange recurring banging noises originating from the second level above them. One of the female employees heard what sounded like furniture or chairs being dragged along the flagstone-tiled floor. When she and her co-workers dashed up the stairway to locate the source of the noise, they found nobody in the tower except themselves. Upon investigation, we noted that there is a set of antique chairs constructed of buckskin deer hide and antlers sitting below the large mural paintings. These chairs are original pieces of furniture chosen and placed in the Watchtower by Mary Colter. If a new employee rearranges the antique chairs, they will soon be "dragged" back to their original location.

Many Grand Canyon National Park employees believe the Watchtower ghost to be that of its designer, Mary Colter. Perhaps she is still perfecting her masterpiece and double-checking to be sure everything is in order and in its proper place.

TUSAYAN RUIN'S
ANCIENT SPIRITS

Traveling three miles west of Desert View Tower, you will find the ancient Tusayan Ruin and museum. Just off the East Rim Drive, a short self-guided trail leads visitors to Tusayan Ruin and a chance to investigate a bit of ancient history. If you have time, take the thirty- to forty-five–minute guided tour given by one of the National Park Service rangers. Why this village was abandoned by the Pueblo Indians remains a mystery. Not only was the Grand Canyon their home, but also it was a sacred place.

The Tusayan museum is located inside a stone building near the walkway. It is dimly lit to protect some of the artifacts on display. The centerpiece of the museum is a group of ancient Native American figures resembling horses. They are made out of twigs and have been dated as being over 4,000 years old.

Stacey Wittig, a journalist who pens an Examiner.com column titled "Grand Canyon National Park Examiner," was enthusiastic to share the history and story of this mysterious village. According to tree-ring dating, construction began on this pueblo in A.D. 1185. The families that lived and died here were ancestors to the Hopi people who now live 100 miles to the east. Once a lively village situated near the Grand Canyon's rim, the pueblo now lies in ghostly ruins.

A second group that lived nearby—the people of the Navajo tribe—called those who once lived at Tusayan Ruin *Anasazi*, which in the Navajo language means "enemy ancestors." To the Hopi people, this word is degrading to their dead forebears. To the Navajo, the word conveys their fear of the dead.

"Navajo people avoid places like Tusayan Ruin because their religion teaches that *Chindi*—or bad spirits—inhabit such ruins," Stacey explained. "Chindi resemble a dust devil and are the ghosts left behind when [an] individual of the Navajo tribe dies. If living people stay near dead bodies, the Chindi, which are made of all that was bad about the deceased persons,will inhabit the bodies of the living, causing Chindi sickness or 'ghost sickness.' Chindi lingers around bodies or possessions of the dead and that is why the dead person's belongings are burned. Further, if a person dies inside a home, tradition dictates that the dwelling be abandoned or burned."

Chindi "ghost sickness" is sometimes associated with witchcraft. Its symptoms include weakness, loss of appetite, feelings of suffocation, reoccurring nightmares, and a constant feeling of terror.

Traditional Navajos avoid dead bodies and places such as Tusayan Ruins where people have died. Although Navajos avoid the Grand Canyon ruins, according to Grand Canyon National Park ranger Erin Huggins, the Zuni and Hopi people still visit Tusayan Ruins and perform religious ceremonies.

"When you go to Tusayan Ruins, look for the small kiva or round ceremonial chamber described on the trail map," Stacey recommended. "Charred timber supports indicate that the small kiva was burned. The last time I was at Grand Canyon National Park, I sat near the small kiva drinking in the aroma of nearby juniper and piñon pine and pondered potential encounters with Chindi spirits. The quiet stillness was disturbed only by the creaking metal hinge on the metal box where visitors were retrieving trail maps. The hair on the back of my head tingled as I felt the dark energy of sadness emanating from the kiva's round, rocky wall. Tracks through the middle of the dirt floor revealed that an elk had recently visited."

Stacey continued, "Croaks of a raven interrupted my meditation and reminded me of recent words recited by Hopi guide James Poley: 'The ruins of the national parks are footprints of our people. We left these places. We left some for good reasons and others for bad reasons.' I held my breath—afraid that I would ingest a lungful of bad spirits—and got up and left Tusayan Ruin."

Stacey Wittig's web site is at www.examiner.com/grand-canyon-national-park-in-national/stacey-wittig.

LEGENDS
OF THE
MULES

The famous mules of the Grand Canyon are somewhat like Hollywood celebrities. Visiting riders and their mules develop uncanny relationships during their ten-mile ride in via Bright Angel Trail to Phantom Ranch, and the eight-mile ride out via the Kaibab Trail. The riders put all their confidence into the beasts that carry them within inches of the narrow trail's edge. The mules and their passengers seem to bond, and the riders never forget their trusty mules' names. After their vacation in Arizona's desert and their Grand Canyon adventure, these travelers return to city life—but they continue to brag about their mules like they were long-lost friends. Maybe it's because they are so grateful their mules trudged up the canyon trail without bucking them over the side.

Some of the riders have sent money to guides and mule skinners to buy extra oats, carrots, and bales of hay for their favorite mules. And, believe it or not, there have been travelers who returned to the canyon several years later requesting to ride the same animal—and they asked for that pack mule by its name!

Unreliable mules once found themselves put out to pasture, and some of them wound up at the glue factory. "SOP" became the acronym, pronounced just as it's spelled, a mule received that nickname for constantly trying to pitch off its load into the canyon below—"Son of a Pitch."

Legend says that, many years ago, there was a "wreck" on the Kaibab Trail when six pack-mules went out into space for their one and only lesson in skydiving. The packer reported all the mules were missing in action except for the mule trusted to carry the delicate eggs for Phantom Ranch's kitchen—"Fallopian." Upon returning to the top of the trail, the packer went into the bunkhouse and did a little bit of paperwork. He transferred that name to a similarly marked mule—then secretly replaced the missing eggs from money out of his own pocket. This way he was still able to collect some extra cash for delivering the eggs.

"Bananas" was another one of the mules said to have lost his footing and fallen from the Kaibab Trail to meet his maker. One Saturday night, the mule packer sat in the "Old Tusayan," the neighborhood bar south of Grand Canyon Village. He was a great storyteller and as you can imagine, his sad story about Bananas' untimely demise held his audience in suspense. Soon the man burst into song and started to sing, "Yes, We Have No Bananas" in honor of Banana's split from the trail. Everyone in the bar began to hoot and holler, and sing along! Of course, all of the bar patrons bought the entertaining mule packer another round of beer at the expense of the ghostly memory of Bananas.

The most famous of all the mules was Bright Angel or "Brighty" as he was nicknamed by mule riders. Brighty gained fame and notoriety in the Marguerite Henry book titled *Brighty of the Grand Canyon*, written in 1953. It may come as a surprise to many of the book's readers that Brighty really did exist. Brighty lived on the North Rim from about 1892 to 1922, and carried water from the spring up to the rim to the tourists arriving at the canyon. The legend says he was the first mule to cross the Kaibab Suspension Bridge and even had helped carry in supplies while the structure was being built.

Author Henry states that most of the characters in her book are real and that the majority of the incidents really did happen. Brighty was the mule that hunted mountain lions in the Grand Canyon with President Theodore Roosevelt. It is also said Brighty helped to solve a mystery in the canyon having to do with his friend and companion, an old prospector. The miner was said to have been murdered by a claim jumper. Brighty searched for the killer and risked everything to bring the criminal to justice.

A bronze statue honoring Brighty has been erected in Grand Canyon Lodge's Sun Room. It was sculpted by the talented Peter Jepsen. Ms. Henry wrote the inscription on the art work.

"The artist captured the soul of Brighty—forever wild, forever free."

In a superstitious custom, guests rub Brighty's nose for good luck when they visit Grand Canyon Lodge. And, from the look of his very shiny nose, Brighty has provided an abundance of good luck and karma through the years.

Some guests and trail guides say you can see the dark shadowy outline of Brighty's small figure climbing the rocky terrain near the Grand Canyon Lodge on moonlit nights... still wild and free.

MULE PACKER MEETS GHOST AT GORDON'S PANEL

The Grand Canyon mule guides have an uncanny way of taking you back to another time when life was a bit easier and the pace so much slower. The group is very tight knit—many of them having worked together on the trails for years. They can certainly tell a yarn or two. But, when it comes to ghost tales, mule runners always tell it straight. They have seen it all.

I spoke to a mule packer who has trotted along the Grand Canyon trails for almost forty years. In addition, he has organized rides at several other national parks. I will call him "Sam Douglas" for privacy reasons. During the off season, Sam, also an avid hiker, often explored the out-of-the-way trails along the North Rim.

"I believe there are ghosts of ancient Indian tribes almost everywhere you walk near the Grand Canyon," Sam told me.

"You can't always see them, but you can feel them close by, watching your every move."

Sam led a group of Grand Canyon visitors on mule-back down to a place not known to very many guests, on the North Rim. Gordon's Panel, also known as Shaman's Gallery, is located near Tuckup and Cottonwood canyons.

"You have to ride quite a ways back on a little-maintained trail," he told me, "Bring plenty of water if you plan to go back there in the summer months or you might become a ghost yourself. Once you arrive at 'Gordon's Panel' you will be awestruck. An overhang about sixty feet along offers an ancient mural of hand-painted 'ghosts.' Some of the ghosts are at least six feet tall."

Sam continued, "I believe the tribes painted what they *saw* down there. This whole area is haunted and I have experienced the ghosts myself."

We sat down outside the mule barn so he could continue his story.

"Once after viewing the Panel I was hiking back to the main camp near Cottonwood Spring. Suddenly, I could feel the hair on my arms and the back of my neck raise, and I felt a cold chill rush through my body. The temperature seemed to drop. I could feel someone following me and hot on my trail. I could hear footsteps getting closer and closer behind me."

Sam shifted in his chair and I could tell he was feeling rather uneasy simply telling his story.

"I turned around and couldn't believe my eyes. Pebbles and rocks on the trail were moving as though some unseen entity was kicking them up as it grew closer and closer to me. Dust was rising up from the dirt trail pathway." His eyes grew big as he described the unexplained phenomenon.

"Whoa!" I raised my eyebrows in amazement.

"I could hear the twigs of the bushes snapping behind me as I hurried along the trail, almost jogging at a quick gait. I could tell *whoever* it was behind me did not want me there. Once I hiked a great distance away from the Panel, it backed off."

"Have you camped down there?" I took a sip from my can of soda.

"Not at the Panel," he told me, "but, we have camped at Cottonwood Spring. Another one of the mule packers and I decided to set up camp there after a long day of hiking and exploring in the area of the Panel. We carefully pitched our tent close to the spring. The temperature dropped and there was a light snowfall. Huddled in our sleeping bags, we began to hear loud footsteps pacing around and around our tent. It was as though someone was agitated and wanted us to leave. We heard large rocks being thrown all around our campsite. Occasionally one of us would pop open the tent flap and wave the flashlight in all directions trying to see who or what was raising such a ruckus. We didn't see anyone or anything. We could hear the heavy–foot-stomping and rock-throwing throughout the night. Neither of us could sleep."

"That must have been a scary night for you both," I nodded.

"The strangest part came in the morning after sunrise, when it was early light, we were finally brave enough to crawl out of the tent. With all that rock throwing there should have been stones lying near our shelter. And, with all that foot-stomping around the tent there was not one foot print in that fresh fallen snow! Nothing!" Sam shook his head. "I truly believe there is some sort of *protector* of Gordon's Panel that makes sure intruders do not bother the spirits there. I think there's an Indian burial ground nearby—hence the ghostly panel drawings."

Sam convinced me that sometime in the future I should bring my paranormal team on a hiking investigation adventure to the Panel. He insisted it would be a ghost hunt we would never forget. Sam advised we should camp close to Cottonwood Spring on the Bureau of Land Management side. He is almost certain the ghosts will return for a visit and bring more than enough evidence for our paranormal files.

GHOSTLY WOMEN OF GRAND CANYON LODGE

The Grand Canyon Lodge complex today consists of a main lodge building, twenty-three deluxe cabins, and ninety-one standard cabins on Bright Angel Point at the North Rim of the Grand Canyon. The lodge seems to back up into the side of the rim, giving visitors a magnificent view of the canyon.

The Union Pacific Railroad announced plans for a lodge on Grand Canyon's more remote North Rim in 1927. They set up construction camps on Bright Angel Point, and building continued right through the winter months. Some of the workmen brought their families with them. A stonemason's wife taught school to children residing on the North Rim during those months.

When completed in 1928, the Grand Canyon Lodge boasted the main lodge building, along with twenty deluxe cabins, and one hundred standard cabins for guests. In the fall of 1932 a devastating fire ignited when sparks flew from one of the lodge's massive fireplaces in the early morning hours. The fire destroyed the main lodge and two of the deluxe cabins. Luckily, there were no injuries or no loss of life. Employees said small plumes of smoke rising from the smoldering stone piers reminded them of ghosts ascending into the sky. The main lodge was rebuilt in 1937 using most of the remnants of the stone foundation, and piers, walls, and chimneys of the original building. The new structure was designed to resemble a rustic hunter's lodge.

The U-shaped lodge building was constructed of Kaibab limestone, ponderosa logs, and log-slab siding on a wooden framework. The main lodge houses a lobby, dining room, recreation room, western-style saloon, sun room, and various offices and hotel facilities. Inside the Grand Canyon Lodge, guests can visit the life-size statue of the legendary mule "Brighty of the Grand Canyon," to rub his shiny nose and take home a little mystical luck.

About ten miles separate the South Rim's Grand Canyon Village from the rural Grand Canyon Lodge on the North Rim. The canyon ravens can cover that distance at ease. But, to travel from one rim to the other by car involves driving around the eastern end of the Grand Canyon and up towards Lee's Ferry. It is a 200-mile drive and takes about five hours to reach Grand Canyon Lodge. The roadways are primitive, and open only from mid-May through mid-October because of the harsh, cold winters.

The North Rim has less traffic and is not as congested at the hotels and look-out areas as its counterpart in Grand Canyon Village on the South Rim. Most visitors to the North Rim come for the solitude, mule trips, hiking, and scenic views.

Vacationing in the remote forests of the North Rim can also become a haunted experience. The lodge is located at the end of the highway—a dead end, so to speak. The forest is thick, and the full moon the only guiding light. Facilities at the North Rim are rather rustic. Many visitors rent cabins in the forest-ringed campgrounds near the Rim Trail. After dark, the North Rim becomes quiet and almost eerie. The night's blackness seems to keep employees and guests close to their quarters.

The name of the ghost of Grand Canyon Lodge is Edith. Nobody is sure of Edith's true identity, but she is rumored to be the wife of one of the workmen who built the structure long ago. The heavy wooden door to the lodge slams shut each time it is accidently left open. Edith has been tagged as the mischievous spirit who insists on keeping this entryway closed. She has been known to rearrange furniture and art displays if they were not to her liking. For example, the art gallery staff once found pottery from a Hopi art show lined up in the middle of the gallery floor.

Bryan Meeks, one of the mule wranglers on the North Rim, witnessed a possible interaction with Edith's ghost at the end of the summer season in 2008. He told me that it normally takes the entire staff about two hours of working together to do the lodge's final closing for the winter season. One of the duties of the staff members is to walk through the lodge and lock every window. Then, storm shutters are closed and secured to protect the windows from snow and freezing temperatures.

"The lodge was cleaned, locked, and the security alarms were set," Bryan recalled. "Everyone climbed into their vehicles and started down the road. Fifteen minutes after we left, the security system was triggered and the alarm company immediately notified the staff manager of an intruder. Everyone turned around and sped back to the Grand Canyon Lodge. When we pulled in front of the lodge, we were dumbfounded to see every storm shutter on the building had been re-opened. Perhaps Edith was not ready for the tourist season to end."

Bryan had been warned about the Grand Canyon Lodge ghosts from the first day he started working as the new mule wrangler. The other wranglers told him how the crew made it a playful practice to blame Edith for any unexplained events that happened on the North Rim.

One morning, Bryan became a true believer in Edith's ghost. He woke up early on a typical work day, stretched, and took his time climbing out of bed. It was still dark out and he knew it would be a couple more hours until the cook had breakfast going down at the wranglers' cook house. He happened to glance out the window and saw someone walking to the cookhouse carrying a lantern. He thought the cook was heading over to get an early start on frying up the breakfast bacon. Later, at breakfast, Bryan spoke to the cook and mentioned he had seen her heading to the cookhouse earlier than usual.

The cook had a puzzled look on her face. "That wasn't me. I came down and started breakfast the same time I always do—I wasn't early at all."

The rest of the wranglers gave Bryan a poke and kidded, "Bryan, we think you just saw your first ghost! You just saw Edith!"

Bryan said he felt like an official member of the crew from that day on.

A hooded apparition gliding along the pathways near the remote forests of the Grand Canyon's North Rim has been nicknamed the "Wandering Woman." She is usually seen wearing a white robe embellished with a small floral design. She always has a scarf over her head. Her head is bowed down toward the ground as she wrings her hands in despair.

Although her identity and story are undocumented, the employees at the Grand Canyon Lodge state that she roams the Rim Trail searching for the family she lost in the canyon many years ago. She supposedly committed suicide in the lodge during the 1920s after learning that her beloved husband and son had been killed in a hiking accident. Even though the first lodge burned down in 1932, the second one reused Kaibab limestone foundation is the perfect element for embracing a residual haunting inside its rock walls.

A gentleman staying at the lodge in the summer of 2007 was taken by surprise when he saw a strange woman standing in the doorway to his room.

"I tried to approach the weeping woman to see if I could help her," he explained. "She seemed deeply troubled as though something was terribly wrong. As I walked closer to her, she vanished before my eyes."

The weeping ghost has also been spotted on Transept Trail. In the evening, her haunting wails of grief echo throughout the canyon. Nobody knows who this mysterious woman might be, as Arizona's death records were not always properly filed in the early years of statehood.

One of the young rangers lived in the Inn Cabins. It was an ideal location—close to his duties on the Rim Trail and the visitor center near Grand Canyon Lodge. One night, just as he was almost asleep, he heard noises outside. He looked at his alarm clock and saw it was about 10:30 P.M. It sounded as though someone was pacing near his cabin. Then he began to hear a woman crying. It was a loud sobbing as though someone was suffering from a deep loss or sorrow. Soon the weeping faded into the darkness and he heard the woman walk away into the woods. The ranger thought about getting up out of bed to investigate, but figured it was only one of the female employees experiencing a bout of loneliness or melancholy.

A few nights later, the wailing began again. This time the ranger sat up in bed and listened. He felt troubled but, same as before, he really didn't want to intrude on someone's private affairs.

One evening he was having a few friends over for a gathering at his cabin. They heard a rap on the door and the room grew very silent. He opened the door to find a young female ranger who lived in a nearby cabin. She was shaking and looked very frightened. She begged the young rangers to come outside and help her find the sobbing woman.

She had heard the wail of a woman near her cabin door, but her dog had become aware of the presence outside her cabin long before the sobbing began. The young female ranger feared for the woman's safety in the darkness. When she opened the cabin door, she saw nobody. Five rangers gathered to do a quick check around the cabins but saw no trace of the woman. Every time they paused to listen, they could hear the weeping becoming softer—as though her spirit was drifting back into the woods. They walked to the canyon's edge together. Looking down the Rim Trail, they saw a glowing white form gliding along the pathway. Suddenly, the spirit made a sharp left and disappeared from sight. The crying ceased. Some employees at the North Rim believe the Wandering Woman is really "La Llorona"—or the wailing woman.

La Llorona is said to have been a beautiful woman who killed her children in order to be with the man she loved, but was subsequently rejected by him. As a result, she killed herself. Upon reaching the gates of heaven, she was asked where her children were. She was not to be allowed into heaven until she found her children. Now she is doomed to wander Earth for all eternity, searching in vain for her murdered offspring. Her constant weeping is the reason for her name. In some versions of the tale, she will kidnap wandering children or those who disobey their parents

Children who come to the Grand Canyon with their families should be advised to stay away from the edge of the North Rim and to listen for the weeping of the ghostly lady in white. Unruly children may have their vacations cut short.

Some of the staff working near the Grand Canyon Lodge believe there is a group of ghostly children who return to play on the swings and merry-go-round of a former playground located where the center courtyard and flagpole stands today. The playground equipment was removed many years ago, but Grand Canyon workers insist they have heard children's voices and laughter coming from an unknown source. They claim to have seen youngsters frolicking on a phantom playground that suddenly dissipates without a trace. It is almost as though they went sliding back into another dimension within the mysterious canyon walls.

Guests at the lodge have noticed their offspring playing or talking with unseen children in the courtyard. The youngsters insisted there were other boys and girls wanting them to stay and play for a while. There are no reports of a group of children dying at the lodge. Spirits often return to a location or a time period of their lives when life was easy and carefree. The playground ghosts are merely reliving happy vacations.

For a truly unique sighting, keep your eyes peeled for a so-called "phantom" Kaibab squirrel with tufted ears, known as the "Silver Ghost of the North Rim." This silver-coated squirrel is not found anywhere else in the world due to the uniqueness of the Kaibab plateau that supports an island of forest surrounded by desert. The "Silver Ghost" often makes a quick dash across the trail pathways, so keep a close watch for this elite creature.

Grand Canyon Lodge, North Rim
Reservations: 877-386-4383 (877-Fun-4-Ever)

HAUNTED
HOUSING

I was very fortunate to contact a young man who recently worked as a Grand Canyon National Park ranger. He was very enthusiastic about a book featuring the legendary canyon ghosts. His paranormal encounter took place about mid-January 2007. Christian Espanol was always happy with the employee housing perk that came with his job as a ranger here, residency in a one-bedroom, single-story duplex inside the park. He called his apartment "the relaxation pad" because all of his friends loved to come over. It quickly became the "hangout" and the popular place to spend their time off. Christian was a bachelor in those days, living all alone—or, at least, that is what he thought.

Espanol was having one of his typical sleepless nights— the kind when you are tired, but just can't seem to relax and fall asleep. He was lying on his living room sofa watching a late-night TV talk show. He finally felt tired enough to try to get some sleep, so he clicked off the remote and made himself comfortable right there. No more than ten minutes after Christian dozed off to sleep, he was awakened by a growling sound that seemed to be coming from the kitchen.

"I had been living in my apartment for a few months and so I was able to identify every sound my house made. This was not like any sound I had ever heard before," Espanol stated.

He decided to investigate. He rose off the sofa and walked toward the kitchen thinking what he had heard was an animal sound. The growling seemed unusual in the consistency of it. There was no variance in tone or pitch—just a constant "grrrrrrrrr" without break or ending. The volume increased as he approached the kitchen. Christian walked cautiously without turning any lights on. The ambient light was more than enough for him to navigate his own apartment in the dark. But, when Espanol reached the entrance of his kitchen, he was looking into total darkness.

"The usual street and moon light that filtered through my kitchen window at night was not there," Christian explained. "However, it was not the darkness that threw me off. The growling was now directly in my face—no more than a foot or two from my nose. Yet, I could not see from where it was coming. I switched on the kitchen light, and saw a flash of a mountain lion pouncing on me with his canines ready to bury deep in my throat! As soon as the light turned on, the growling stopped."

Christian still believed there was an animal in his house, and not anything of the supernatural. He opened his refrigerator, the freezer, and all of the cupboards expecting to have a mountain lion or raccoon attack him. When nothing appeared—not even in the disorganized Tupperware cup-board—he decided the source of the growl had either gone away or it was just his imagination. Espanol flicked off the kitchen light and walked back to the sofa. As he lay down the menacing growl came back as a deafening roar. Now wide awake, Christian stood up and starting turning on every light in the apartment, including the porch light. The sound was coming from every room in the small living space. It was loud and constant no matter which room he stood in.

Espanol suddenly wondered if he might have a ghost in his apartment. He was standing in his bedroom contemplat-ing what he should do next just as the growling abruptly ended once again. At this point, Christian was scared out of his wits. His mind was racing as he tried to prepare his next plan of action. After several minutes of silence, he decided to sit on the sofa, turn the TV back on and wait for the sun to come up. He left on every light in the apartment, knowing there was no use in trying to sleep that night.

As Christian walked toward the sofa, he glanced at some shelves he had installed when he first moved in. He was not looking at anything particular on the shelves—they were just on the way to the sofa. Suddenly a haunting melody began to play near the shelf closest to the living room.

"I stood completely still," Christian recalled. "I kept glancing around the room trying to figure out the source of this new sound in the night. The slow-paced, hypnotizing music was vaguely familiar to me. My eyes finally focused on an ornamental figurine that was given to me by friends when I lived in Japan. I had completely forgotten that the figurine, a rabbit dressed in a kimono, played music. The musical rabbit had been placed on a high shelf and un-touched since the time I set it there after moving in. Before that, it had been stored away in its original packaging box. It had traveled with me from Japan to England, and then on to the United States."

Now, when Christian tried to wind up the musical figurine, its works resisted. Whatever had caused the figurine to activate had his undivided attention. Christian stood in silence for several minutes and tried to take in what had just happened. He eventually sat back down on the sofa and turned the TV to a late night infomercial. He thought this whole episode seemed like something he had watched before in a slasher horror movie. As the sun began to rise, Christian made a deal with his mysterious new roommate.

"This is my house. I live here, like it or not!" he said firmly. "I obviously rub off on you the wrong way, and you are not exactly *my* favorite thing right now, either. I spend most of my time in my living room, so you can stay in my bedroom until you find the need to go someplace else—but *you* are the one that is going to have to go."

The growling roommate has never made its presence known again since that night. Christian later shared the apartment with his girlfriend. Some nights they were awakened by strange noises or feelings, but they were never disturbed as he had been on that one winter night. Perhaps when Christian Espanol took a stand against the unknown, the invisible force accepted him as a friend rather than an enemy.

EXTRA RESIDENTS IN MARY COLTER'S DORMS

E mployees with the Grand Canyon National Park Service and Xanterra Parks and Resorts are provided with housing in various facilities throughout the park. They live in dormitories, apartments, and even mobile homes.

Many of the single women reside in the Colter Hall Dorms that nestle on a slope just behind El Tovar Hotel. These rooms have been used for generations of employees since they opened in 1937.

The Colter Hall Dorms for women was designed by Mary Colter, as a stone construction that blends with the foundation of El Tovar. The seventy-five-room structure includes a common room centered near a large fireplace.

Construction of Colter Hall Dorm required removing four older buildings, including a laundry and a photography studio. Are ghosts from these former businesses haunting the present-day dormitories?

Isabelle, who worked in one of the South Rim shops, was one of the people living at the Colter Hall Dorms, assigned to Room 4.

"Years ago, a friend of my parents was actually assigned to the same dorm room I have," Isabelle told us. "I don't know if she ever encountered the ghosts, but I sure have!"

Isabelle explained that living in the small efficiency rooms is much like living in typical college dorms. Two women share the same room that barely has space for two twin beds. Each room has two closets to store their personal items, and a shared bathroom is down the hall.

Isabelle strategically situated her bed near the room door.

"One night in the spring of 2010 we saw a ghost of a man go in and out of the closet," she said breathlessly. "I remember he was dressed in early 1900s clothing. It was as though he was wearing a security or railroad uniform."

The roommates always locked their door from the inside when they were ready to call it a night. But, many times, they found the door not only unlocked, but also wide open the following morning.

The women at Colter Hall Dorms have heard loud, continuous scratching noises coming from deep inside the closed closets. When the residents opened the closets to investigate, they did not see anything physical—but not all ghosts manifest into full apparitions. The scraping sounds could easily be attributed to canyon critters, but on the other hand, could there still be former Grand Canyon employees entering in and out of an unseen portal?

Another girl who lived in the dorms recalled how she and her co-worker would remove the window screen and place day-old bagels on the ledge to tempt the large ravens that soar over the South Rim. She enjoyed watching them swoop down from the ponderosa pines and hearing their wings flap in the breeze. After the co-worker ended her life in 1998 by jumping into the canyon near the vortex at the Worship Site, Isabelle remembered the ravens frantically cawing the next day and following her wherever she went in the village.

"Sometimes there is a sense of weirdness that surrounds the canyon," she sighed. "Can't explain it, but it is there."

A resident at the adjacent Victor Hall for men told a similar story. Another Mary Colter creation, this dorm was built during the same time period as Colter Hall. The young man was off work for the afternoon and taking a little cat nap on his bed. His roommate had quietly entered the room to use the bathroom. Out of the corner of his eye, he could see the roommate in the other room. Standing at the foot of the bed was a man. The man stared at him with a confused look on his face. He was an older fellow, and was wearing a plaid flannel shirt, suspenders, and a weathered old hat. At first the young man thought it was a new employee who was lost and entered the wrong room by mistake, or someone assigned to the same room in error. He sat up, rubbed his eyes, and asked the bewildered man if he was lost. The specter vanished in front of his eyes.

Colter Hall and Victor Hall are employee residences and not open to the public, but perhaps if you or someone you know resides there, you could experience a roommate from another dimension in time.

GRAND CANYON
PIONEER
CEMETERY

The Grand Canyon Pioneer Cemetery is located on the South Rim of the Grand Canyon in Grand Canyon National Park, just a little west of the Shrine of Ages church. The cemetery is maintained by the American Legion Grand Canyon Post #42 and is still in use today. Burials are limited to canyon residents who must meet certain qualifications and have the permission of the park superintendent. To qualify, the individual must have lived at the Grand Canyon for no fewer than three years, and must have made a substantial contribution to the development of, public knowledge about, or understanding and appreciation for Grand Canyon National Park.

Visitors to this cemetery will find many familiar names among the tombstones, names featured in the canyon's vast history. Some of these pioneers lived long lives right here, others lived or worked here for periods of time and kept a special piece of the area in their hearts. It is virtually a "who's who" of Grand Canyon history and contains roughly 304 burial plots.

One of the gravestone memorials tells of the tragedy of the airline crash of June 30, 1956. When a TWA Constellation and a United Airlines DC-7 collided over the eastern part of the Grand Canyon, 128 passengers and crew died. The planes both left Los Angeles about the same time and were traveling east. They eventually collided into each other at about 20,000 feet elevation. At the time, the accident was named the worst airline disaster on record and it, along with the increasing use of jet airlines, led to major changes in the duties of a federal agency dating from 1926, the ancestor of today's safety-monitoring Federal Aviation Administration. The remains of twenty-nine passengers were never identified. They were respectfully buried in the Grand Canyon Cemetery.

Other noted pioneers buried in the cemetery include:

John Hance was one of the South Rim's first residents, a prospector and tour operator. Hance was known for telling tall tales and always had an interesting story about life in the canyon. He died in Flagstaff, Arizona, in 1919. His friends buried him in a secluded rustic spot about a mile east of Grand Canyon Village. A few weeks later, Congress created Grand Canyon National Park. The National Park Service began a program of civic improvements, and named John Hance's grave as the beginning of the first village cemetery. When you are there, take a look at his headstone and his footstone. Notice the distance? Friends placed the stones several extra feet apart as a reference to Hance's reputation for telling his humorous *tall* tales.

William Henry Ashurst was a Flagstaff resident and another of the canyon prospectors from the 1880s. He died in a landslide near the Colorado River below the Grand Canyon Village. Ashurst's friend, John Hance, buried him near the landslide. He was disinterred twice, and finally buried in the Grand Canyon Cemetery.

The cemetery holds the remains of many canyon pioneers, park employees, and village residents who have passed on through the years, including *Emery Kolb, Pete Berry, Ralph Cameron* and early Park Superintendent *M. R. Tillotson.*

William Wallace Bass has only a memorial monument next to his wife Ada. He chose for his ashes to be spread over the mystical Holy Grail Temple by airplane after his death in 1933.

Roy and Edna May Lemmons met when she worked at the canyon as a Harvey Girl. At the end of the season, Edna was broken-hearted when it was time for her to return home. But, to Edna's surprise, Roy showed up on her doorstep on a spooky Halloween evening to propose. They were soon married, and lived a long life together. They are united in death and buried in the Grand Canyon Cemetery.

The cemetery is a quiet, restful place visited by residents and tourists alike. Guests have noted an eerie presence as they enter the cemetery gate, a presence that seems to follow them throughout the grounds. Maybe it is only the rustling of the pine trees that seem to echo the whisper-like chatter of the spirits, the constant breeze running through the boughs.

People often associate a cemetery with ghosts and hauntings, and the Grand Canyon Pioneer Cemetery is no exception. So, why would a ghost haunt this spot? Think about your relatives or loved ones who have passed on. We most likely know which cemetery they are buried in and this would be the place we would go to visit them, bring flowers and other tributes, and talk to them. While we are in the cemetery, we are putting out a lot emotional energy. This energy could draw the spirits to us.

Sometimes a cemetery becomes somewhat of a social gathering point. The Grand Canyon Pioneer Cemetery is very beautiful setting. After a visit from tourists and relatives, the spirits many decide to stay around for a while and enjoy the scenery.

It is also the spirits' only connection to life in this world. The headstone may be the only memory of them we still have. So even though one might not "see" a ghost in the Grand Canyon cemetery, it is certainly a place a spirit can visit on the off chance of being noticed, if only emotionally.

No doubt a few of these former Grand Canyon pioneers are still hiking to the depths of the canyon and back to the rim on a regular basis!

MYSTERIOUS GRAVES ON THE SOUTH RIM

A few of the employees at the Grand Canyon South Rim know of secret grave sites tucked away in the hillsides and other places not obvious to casual observers. Not just anybody can be buried in the national park, but I do suspect there have been hundreds of urns brought to viewing points by loved ones. The ashes are secretly scattered in the wind, and eventually settle deep down into the cavernous tomb.

For years there has been a story circulating that a former Harvey Girl is buried in a grave across the street from El Tovar near the guest parking lot. Many a new Grand Canyon employee will tell you the stories of the reported sightings of a black-caped ghostly figure resembling a woman. It has been seen late at night walking along the pathway leading up from the steps, just to the right of El Tovar Hotel. Staying along the path, the mysterious phantom, believed to be the Harvey Girl, passes by the gravestone and disappears behind the Hopi House.

There actually is a stone maker that looks suspiciously like a tombstone directly across the street from El Tovar. It is hard to spot if you don't know where to look. Passing vehicles and guests on foot may have assumed the stone monument of "Pirl Ward" was merely a utility access marker. Pedestrians rarely notice the polished slab as it is not very visible under the shady trees and landscaping.

The tombstone also is weather-damaged, making it difficult to read the words inscribed. Wiping off the stone with a soft cloth, one can make out the name, "Pirl A. Ward" and the years "1879-1934."

Now, with a name like Pirl A. Ward one might speculate this is a woman or former Harvey Girl of El Tovar. Some have even suggested that Pirl A. Ward was a former lover of Fred Harvey. Although the theory makes a great romantic ghost story, the El Tovar staff has verified that Pirl Adelbert Ward was actually a man and a veteran of the Spanish American War.

Mr. Ward's grandson, William Ward, stated that his grandfather was the building contractor during El Tovar's construction, and owned a carpentry shop in Williams, Arizona. This explained why a gravestone marker would be placed close to the El Tovar...but is it a real grave? William Ward confirmed his grandfather Pirl moved to California to live out his final years. He died in 1934 and is buried in Artesia, California.

The marker was placed near the hotel by friends in nearby Williams, to honor the elder Ward's role in Grand Canyon history as a builder of El Tovar. This doesn't mean the mysterious black-caped figure scurrying along the El Tovar

pathways is not real. Perhaps someone will be able to identify her in the future.

Farther west along the Rim Trail are the graves of two
prominent Grand Canyon residents and their faithful pet
canine. Charles and Olga Brant are buried near Hermit Road
on the South Rim. The Brants were the first caretakers of El
Tovar Hotel. Charles and Olga requested that, upon their
deaths, they be buried in a spot in the Grand Canyon where
they could overlook El Tovar for all eternity. It is rare that
anyone is buried outside the Grand Canyon Cemetery on
national park land, but this was a very special circumstance.
The deceased couple had been well liked and respected residents in Grand Canyon Village.

Olga passed away in 1920, and Charles followed a year
later in December 1921. The Brants left behind their faithful
Airedale named "Razzle Dazzle." The Grand Canyon Village
community cared for the pampered canine until he died in
1928. Razzle Dazzle was respectfully placed in a grave near
his owners.

Finding these graves can be rather tricky. We recently
trekked out to hike the South Rim trail and pay our respects
to the Brant family. After you pass Kolb Studio, head toward
the Hermit's Rest Exchange shuttle stop, where the Red Line
and Blue Line buses meet. Go down a few steps and onto
the Rim Trail. After a five- or six-minute walk you will pass
the Rim Worship Site area on your right. Continue along the
trail about for two or three minutes longer. Look up to your
left. About halfway up the steep portion of the trail you will
see a faint trail on the left side. Take this trail, which swoops
back in the direction you came, and start looking for the
grave monuments. They are hidden behind trees and rocks
just below the South Rim.

The isolated graves are enclosed by a large rock wall. You will see a large vertical memorial made of stone with the information of Charles and Olga in front of it. "Razzle Dazzle's" grave is in the far left corner of the site.

The main marker reads:

Charles Brant 1921
His Wife Olga 1920
"In this place doubt is impossible, else why all these wonders,
this surpassing beauty, this grandeur, this deep peace,
this confident repose? No, here is the spirit of God,
here one must believe."
C.A. Brant

The text of Razzle Dazzle's marker reads:

Faithful and beloved Airedale Pet of Mr. and Mrs. Brant
August 16, 1928

Hikers who have gone to look for these graves along the South Rim Trail have said that at times when they thought they had become lost, a large Airedale has appeared and led them to the graves. When they reached the hidden tombstones, the dog vanished. Is this the ghost of Razzle Dazzle still looking out for his masters?

Several Grand Canyon employees tried to give us directions to the grave site. One of them added that we would be walking though the Phantom Fault—or vortex. A vortex is a funnel shape created by a whirling fluid or by the motion of spiraling energy. They are made of anything that flows, such as wind, water, electricity—any energy coming from the Earth.

The Phantom Fault is still active. Guests at the rim can often feel what seems like earthquake movement. The faultline that created the Grand Canyon faults is a fracture in the Earth's crust along which movement occurs. Rarely can anyone see a fault—but you can see evidence of it.

Not many hikers know this energy field exists along the Rim Trail. It is not far from the Rim Worship Site. Many visitors come to bask in the vortex to be vitalized with energy, or for healing purposes. In our search for the Brants' grave, we walked smack into the vortex tucked into the fault line, and experienced a sensation of being off balance as we crossed through the small vortex area. One of us even suddenly felt a bad headache coming on. Look for the obvious change in the landscape as you walk up the hill on the Rim Trail. It is no wonder the Brants selected this powerful section of the Grand Canyon for interment.

THE HEART
OF THE
CANYON

The Grand Canyon is a hauntingly romantic place. Many couples come here to escape their busy lives and schedules and spend quality time with each other. Newlyweds choose to spend their honeymoon at one of the many historic, rustic lodges. Often employees assigned to duties at the Grand Canyon fall in love, and become what they call "Canyon Couples." A former ranger, Christian, said that "there might not be any one object that encapsulates the romantic tendencies of the park like the Heart of the Canyon."

The story of the Heart of the Canyon unfolds an interesting mystery. The majority of couples strolling along the Rim Trail don't notice the pulsating energy that emits from the heart-shaped stone. It is located near the patio area of El Tovar, adjacent to the lounge, and near the path where thousands of guests pass each day. The Heart of the Canyon is a valentine-shaped rock embedded in the Rim Trail wall. Once you locate the heart, you will be facing west toward Lookout Studio. The heart is easy to miss because most visitors on the Rim Trail are in awe of the wonderful canyon views.

There could be many reasons for the stone's placement, but the romantic young ranger had this story to tell. It has been said that during construction of the Rim Trail Wall, one workmen met a beautiful young Harvey Girl employed at El Tovar. They fell deeply in love. Although the Harvey Girl was smitten by the rugged construction worker, she was also pursued by a powerful and wealthy gentleman. When the distinguished suitor learned of the relationship between the Harvey Girl and the handsome laborer, he was outraged. He threatened the vulnerable young woman to end her new romance, or he would step in and end it for her!

Not wanting anything to happen to her love, she reminded the workman that while she was employed as a Harvey Girl, she was under a strict contract for one year, and lawfully could not be seen with him until the binding agreement was completed. The stonemason was heartbroken. Desperately in love, he incorporated a heart-shaped rock into the wall facing El Tovar. Whenever the Harvey Girl looked out of the window, the Heart of the Canyon would be a constant reminder of his love. He felt nothing was impossible to a valiant heart.

One of the housekeepers at the El Tovar spoke of a strange incident she witnessed while finishing up her rooms on the second floor.

"I looked down the hallway and saw a young lady dressed in one of those Harvey Girl uniforms—like you see in the old photographs," said Maria, the housekeeper, as she leaned on her vacuum cleaner. "She had her back to me and was gazing out the window looking down at the Grand Canyon. I kept walking toward her, carrying an armload of towels. When I was about ten feet away from her, her image became all fuzzy and she just faded away. I've only seen her once—but I bet she was the Harvey Girl smitten by the stone layer. When I looked out the window, I could see the Heart of the Canyon in full view."

Another park employee reported that she and her boyfriend often sit at the Heart of the Canyon and chat after work.

"It's just a peaceful setting and close to the dorms," she smiled. "One time we were sitting along the wall at sunset. I just happened to look up at the El Tovar and I saw a sadlooking woman staring down at us from an upstairs window. Jokingly, I told my boyfriend it must be the ghost of the Harvey Girl looking for her lost love. He proposed on the spot!"

The next time you are at the Grand Canyon, keep a watchful eye for the Heart of the Canyon. Sit down along the wall with your loved one and feel the emotional energy left behind by the spirits of the former Harvey Girl and her workman. Ask someone to take your picture. Keep your feet on the ground, but let your heart soar as high as it will.

THE LOOKOUT'S PLAYFUL POLTERGEISTS

The Lookout Studio on the South Rim Trail is also known simply as "The Lookout." It is another of the six Grand Canyon buildings designed by Mary Colter. The stone landmark uses Colter's signature rustic style of architecture, with jagged natural rocks to blend into the environment—in this case, The Lookout was created to match native Pueblo style.

It was constructed in 1914 as a photo studio planned to compete with Kolb Studio farther down the trail. The building was used as an observation point and a resting place for early-day travelers arriving by train. It had a fireplace, art room, and lounge. The large windows presented magnificent views of the Grand Canyon in every direction. High-powered telescopes on the outside terrace offered close-up views of Indian Gardens and the Bright Angel Trail.

Just a short distance from Bright Angel Lodge, Lookout Studios now operates as a gift shop and observation deck for Grand Canyon visitors.

Isabelle, an employee at Lookout Studios, believes the old gift shop has a few playful ghosts that enter the store unseen late at night. Employees closing the shop each evening painstakingly stock the shelves, straighten the merchandise, and sweep up so that everything is prepared for opening hour the following day. Nevertheless, the morning staff often discovers merchandise moved from one display to another, or the books in total disarray.

Isabelle said the fireplace room is especially active. Employees have come in the morning to find the pottery rearranged on the display table or standing upright below it on the floor. They have found popular Grand Canyon books that were showcased on the fireplace mantle knocked over, or scattered everywhere on the tiled floor surface. There have been no signs of animal droppings that would suggest canyon critters might be the culprits.

Mary Colter was known to be very particular about the way her buildings were decorated. Art work and merchandise had to be properly displayed. Could the spirit be Mary Colter demanding the merchandise in the shop be placed for the best sales presentation? Or could it be the ghost of one of the Kolb brothers sneaking into the complex late at night to play a few pranks on what was once their biggest rival? The clerks all agree there is a good energy in the shop and invite visitors to stop in, check out the gifts, and enjoy The Lookout as travelers of the past have done for decades.

KOLB'S STUDIO SPECTER

Kolb Studio sits on the side of the cliff near Bright Angel Trail on the South Rim of the Grand Canyon. It was the home, photography studio, and lab of canyon pioneers Emery and Ellsworth Kolb. Construction on the home began in 1904 with two major additions added over a hundred-year period.

Ellsworth Kolb came to the canyon in 1901. His younger brother, Emery, arrived the following year. They founded their photography studio at the Bright Angel Trailhead in 1902—seventeen years before the creation of Grand Canyon National Park. At first the Kolbs operated in nothing more than a small cave in the side of the canyon wall. The cave served as a makeshift darkroom and lab. Construction on their first permanent structure began in 1904. The crude darkroom was replaced by a two-story wooden structure built on a rock shelf blasted out of the canyon wall.

The Kolb brothers made Grand Canyon history in 1912 by completing a boat trip down the Colorado River. They documented their adventure with a cumbersome movie camera. After they completed a trans-continental movie promotional tour, the brothers returned to the Grand Canyon.

The Kolbs constructed a three-story addition for living quarters and a small showroom in 1915. This addition allowed them to screen the movie of their river trip for Grand Canyon visitors. In fact, Emery presented the movie daily from 1915 until his death in 1976, making it the longest running documentary movie of its kind in the world. Recorded narration was added in 1932, although Emery regularly was on hand to introduce the movie in person.

Most of the photographs the Kolbs sold showed visitors astride Grand Canyon mules. Getting these images was not always an easy task. The only clean water—needed to develop the prints—was located at Indian Gardens, a four-and-a-half-mile hike down Bright Angel Trail. The mule trains were first photographed and later passed by a little man running with a pack full of glass plates in route to the nearest water. Hours later, as the mules made their way back up the trail, they were again passed by the same little man—either Emery or Ellsworth—racing up the trail with the finished prints. This was a daily occurrence until 1932 when water finally became available on the South Rim.

The relationship between Emery and Ellsworth was never very strong. Once Emery married Blanch Bender in 1905, the friction grew. Emery began to spend more time at home with his wife and daughter. The business partnership between the Kolb brothers ended in the summer of 1924. They flipped a coin to determine which brother would leave the canyon. Emery won the coin toss and the rights to the studio. Ellsworth moved to California and received a monthly allotment as a settlement. He died in Los Angeles in 1960 and was buried in the Grand Canyon Pioneer Cemetery.

The last major addition to the Kolbs' studio was made in 1926, when the auditorium and darkroom were expanded. The structure is now five stories high and houses twenty-three rooms. It is listed on the National Register of Historic Places.

The Fred Harvey Company attempted to run Emery Kolb out of business by constructing the nearby Lookout Studio. Lookout Studio, along with a new mule corral, blocked access to Kolb Studio. Many people even visited Lookout Studio mistaking it for Kolb Studio.

At one time the National Park Service tried to rid the canyon of Emery Kolb and what they called an eyesore of a building. Emery stood firm (as did his studio) and continued taking pictures and showing his movie. Emery died in a Flagstaff hospital in 1976 at the age of ninety-five. He was laid to rest next to his wife Blanche and his brother Ellsworth in Pioneer Cemetery in Grand Canyon National Park. Some visitors believe the spirit of this great pioneer is still tending to Kolb Studio and its grounds.

Two months after Kolb's death in 1976, a skeleton was found in Emery's garage by his nephew. Although nobody knew the identity of the unfortunate bones, the manner of death was quite obvious. There was a bullet hole in the temple of the skull. It is believed to be the remains of a distraught hiker found at Shoshone Point in the 1930s. Emery used to assemble the skeleton on the dining room table as if it was some sort of macabre jigsaw puzzle—just to amuse his guests. Emery had a quirky sense of humor that sometimes shocked his friends.

In the beginning it was suspected that this could be the skeleton remains of Glen Hyde, who disappeared without a trace with his new wife Bessie during their 1928 honeymoon rafting trip down the Colorado River. Kolb was the last one to see them alive.

Later it was learned that Ranger Gus Williamson discovered the skeleton in 1933 on Shoshone Point along with some tattered clothing and a .32 revolver. The suicide victim had put a bullet to his right temple sometime earlier that year. Emery Kolb often sat on the coroner's juries for death inquests in the canyon, and somehow acquired the remains of the unknown man and stored them in his garage. The skeleton's moniker may still be a mystery, but at least we know where it came from and what year it was found.

Virginia, the gift shop/gallery manager, has worked at Kolb Studios in the Grand Canyon for several years. Although she has not witnessed a ghost herself, she has overheard many comments from canyon visitors who have had encounters with unexplained ghostly sightings.

The Kolbs' living quarters were in the basement area of the complex, including Emery Kolb's darkroom. Virginia occasionally brings her pet dog to keep her company when she is closing the shop alone late at night. Her faithful pooch refuses to set a paw on the stairs that lead down to the onetime living quarters. He would rather sit at the top of the landing whimpering until Virginia's return.

Virginia recalled an attractive Filipino woman visiting the Grand Canyon in 2009 who witnessed what she believes was Emery Kolb's ghost. The woman saw an elderly gentleman walking down to the short trail just outside the door of the gift shop. It is a private entrance that leads down to the lower levels of the building. When the woman glanced his way a second time, the man had vanished.

Finding this very odd, the woman came back into the shop and told Virginia what she had just witnessed. The man she encountered was dressed as though he was heading to work and wearing a flannel shirt. Virginia grabbed a book off the shelf and flipped to a page with a photograph of the daring and dashing Kolb brothers.

"That's him!" the woman pointed to the page and tapped on the picture of Emery Kolb. Emery was dressed for some formal occasion in the photograph, but there was no mistaking that it was indeed the same man.

The gallery room where Emery Kolb showed his famous Colorado River rafting movie is the location of another ghostly sighting. Kolb has been seen standing at the top of the stairway—just as he did whenever he was preparing to introduce his movie.

"There is no 'spooky' haunting here," Virginia confirmed. "Just a peaceful energy of a spirited old man who loved his home and the Grand Canyon with all his heart."

HERMIT'S REST
& ITS
GHOSTLY AURA

Hermit's Rest was built in 1914 at the west end of Hermit Road in the Grand Canyon Village. The main structure was designed by Southwest architect Mary Colter. Hermit's Rest is the shuttle stop farthest to the west along the South Rim, and provides shade, a fantastic view, and a snack bar and gift shop.

It was originally built as a rest area for tourists riding coaches operated by the Fred Harvey Company on their way to Hermit Camp. The building was designed to be a natural stone formation matching the surrounding landscape.

Colter studied the history of local miners who guided Grand Canyon visitors down into the inner canyon camps. She envisioned the setting as a prospector's cave carved into the rocky hillside. The interior design is indeed cave-like and is highlighted by a huge fireplace set into the back wall. The fireplace has an unusual center stone. It is large, face-like, and almost ghostly.

Mary Colter imagined the rest stop through the eyes of Louis Boucher, known as the Canadian hermit of the Grand Canyon. Boucher was said to wear a white beard, ride a white mule, and tell white lies. Colter's design took guests beneath an archway of jumbled stones that seemed ready to topple over at any minute. An old mission bell, which Colter acquired from an unknown location in New Mexico, hangs beneath the arch. Spirits of the monks are rumored to have become attached to the bell, and followed it to the Grand Canyon.

A lantern dangles from one of the stones, symbolizing a beacon to guide the old hermit, or weary travelers, back to the homestead. If you look closely at night, you may be able to see the ghost of the monk or the old hermit standing at the glowing lantern.

The structure seems to be hidden into the hillside. The porch's log beams are supported by posts constructed from tree trunks with their bark and limbs carefully removed. Rustic furniture inside the building was cut from twisted tree stumps and hollowed-out logs, then placed strategically near the huge arched fireplace.

Mary Colter looked at Hermit's Rest as sort of her very own macabre, ghostly haunted house to decorate. It is said she had cobwebs brought in to hang in the dim corners. She personally helped with rubbing soot into the rocks above the fireplace to make the building look older and more rustic. Some of the workmen had a difficult time understanding Colter's methods of design and even offered to help clean it up. Colter was quoted to say, "You can't imagine what it cost to make it look this old." All this added another dimension to the romantic and haunting aura with which Colter liked to embellish her buildings.

Superstition says you can't leave Hermit's Rest without ringing the old mission bell. Take seven steps past the bell and toss a pebble over your shoulder without looking back. If you hit the bell, you will have seven years of amazingly good luck.

The Hermit Trail extends to the Colorado River and begins about a quarter mile beyond the shuttle stop. Hermit's Rest is the end of the line for the Rim Trail on the western side.

EL TOVAR'S EXTRA VISITORS

The South Rim of the Grand Canyon was first promoted as a destination resort where guests could spend an entire season exploring the canyon's wonders. The Sante Fe Railroad felt it was obligated to provide adequate lodging, so they commissioned the building of El Tovar. The building style is a little bit Swiss chalet, vaguely Scandinavian villa, and also resembles a rustic hunting lodge.

Originally the lodge was to be named Bright Angel Tavern. Michael J. Riordan of Flagstaff campaigned to name the next Harvey House hotel in honor of Spanish conquistador Pedro de Tobar, who first explored the canyon in 1540. Fearing it would be mispronounced and sounding like *"going to the bar,"* Riordan suggested the "Tovar" spelling. By the time the building was completed in 1905, it had been officially

renamed El Tovar in honor of Pedro de Tobar of the Coro-
nado expedition—another confusing element with the Swiss
Norwegian design.

El Tovar opened on January 14, 1905, under the direction of the Fred Harvey Company. It is built just 20 feet from
the edge of the Grand Canyon. The rock and building materials are local, helping El Tovar to blend in with the landscape. The ceiling beams were brought over from Santa Fe,
New Mexico. Charles Whittlesey was the designing architect. What started out to be modest accommodations ended
up having 100 rooms and was considered one of the most
elegant hotels west of the Mississippi.

Mary Colter was called upon to help decorate the interior. She emphasized the natural rustic setting by adorning
the rooms with Indian artifacts and wild game trophies on
the walls of the lobby entryway.

Many say that the private dining room at El Tovar,
built in 1906, was designed especially for President Theodore Roosevelt. The president was known for arriving at the
hotel still dressed in his muddy boots and dusty riding attire. He visited El Tovar in 1914 while he wrote one of his
books about hunting and wilderness adventures. Some of
the moose and buffalo heads displayed on the walls were
shot by Roosevelt.

The Grand Canyon was dedicated as a national park in
April 1920 and El Tovar was proud to host the festivities. It
was a two-day event that included a pilgrimage, to Power
Monument, headed by a group of Hopi people.

El Tovar had a reputation of presenting grand meals to
the guests. They hired the best chefs from around the world
as well as a group of professional kitchen assistants. In order
to be more self-sufficient in such an isolated area, the hotel

kept a small milking barn, and boasted its own bakery and butcher shop.

The famous Harvey Girls staffed El Tovar and helped to civilize the Wild West and the Grand Canyon area. Many of the region's prominent families are descendants of former Harvey Girls.

El Tovar is said to be the favorite place to encounter the ghost of Fred Harvey. His famous Harvey House locations fed and housed rail travelers all over the Southwest. A formal portrait of Harvey adorns El Tovar's grand staircase overlooking the lobby. Employees say that during the winter holidays, sounds of laughter and gala revelry are heard upstairs. Of course, upon inspection, there are no celebrations in progress. Fred Harvey's ghost has been seen wearing a long dark coat and a tall black hat on the third floor during these holiday romps.

There is a very strong Native American presence on the land where the hotel was built. Many guests have reported seeing a mysterious black-caped figure roaming outside El Tovar. They watch it materialize from the pathway leading up the steps just to the right of the hotel. The dark shadowy figure crosses the walkways and seems to disappear into the darkness behind Hopi House.

A Grand Canyon guest named Matt chose El Tovar and the canyon as the perfect place to get engaged. He wasn't counting on a visit from an El Tovar ghost.

"I went to the Grand Canyon and stayed at El Tovar the Saturday after Thanksgiving just so I could propose to my girlfriend. We stayed on the third floor. At about 4:00 in the morning there was a very loud crash in the room. It made me jolt out of bed because it was so loud. It came from the direction of the room where the heater was. The heater never made that sound earlier when we arrived, and we never heard the loud crash again. It was just very startling and totally inexplicable. I looked around the room and there seemed to be nothing out of place or knocked down. It was just a really loud crash we could never explain. We both felt an eerie presence in the room and knew it had to be a visit from a ghost."

A guest named Mary woke up and saw a dark figure of a young woman standing in a corner and staring down at the bed. She told me, "I couldn't make out what she was wearing. The image seemed gray—almost transparent—and it disappeared after a few seconds.

"At first, I thought it was my sister. I quickly glanced over to the other bed and saw that she was sound asleep. When I looked back at the corner of the room, the ghost was gone. I didn't feel threatened. My sister and I stayed in a suite with a balcony on the third floor."

Another vacationing couple registered at El Tovar one Halloween night and didn't even realize they were checking into a haunted hotel.

"We stayed at El Tovar for one night. We checked into a room on the lower terrace level. The room was small but very charming. It looked like it had been part of some fairly recent renovations," the gentleman said.

"The hotel lobby is rustic and pretty cool to just take in the scenery and décor for a while. We also enjoyed the lounge and the back porch. Deer are usually around and you can get pretty close to them," the man chuckled.

He glanced at his wife and his demeanor took on a more serious note.

"About one o'clock in the morning my wife was awakened by someone running their finger across her lips. She looked over at me, but I was sound asleep on the other side of the bed. She shrugged it off and went back to sleep. A short time later, someone grabbed the toe of her foot which was sticking out from under the covers. She could feel the presence of someone standing next to her. She could not move for quite some time out of fear. After a spell she felt brave enough to get up and go to the bathroom. She returned to bed and drifted back to sleep until sunrise."

The traveler adjusted the brim of his cap and continued his story.

"I guess the heating/air conditioning unit in the room was so loud that I just slept through the whole paranormal visit. It must have helped deaden any other ghostly noises in our room. It certainly made for a strange night! My wife told me about her eerie encounter the next morning when we were checking out of the hotel and getting ready to go hiking. I immediately told the desk clerk what happened. She apologized but admitted it was not unusual to hear ghost stories from the guests. These visits have been known to occur in various rooms throughout the hotel. In talking to other hotel guests on our shuttle drive, we learned El Tovar is known to be a haunted hotel. We had no idea before we made our reservation...maybe that was a good thing."

The kitchen and the lounge seem to be two of the more paranormally active areas. One of the young staff waiters told of his experience in the hotel restaurant.

"I have lived and worked at El Tovar for a total of two years in various intervals. The restaurant is said to be quite haunted. One evening I could feel someone pushing the back end of my giant, oval serving tray upward to where I almost lost the six silver metal dish covers and meals. I turned around to see if anyone noticed my reaction, but nobody saw a thing. There was nobody behind me. I didn't know what to think of it."

Another employee reported that he saw a huge ball of light push the kitchen doors open and float across the dining room. It exited through a closed window and disappeared as it soared in the direction of the Grand Canyon.

El Tovar bar and cocktail lounge seems to be another area of the hotel where guests see spirits of the paranormal kind. The lounge was the scene of a deadly confrontation of a park visitor and a Grand Canyon employee. On June 8, 1984, a Fred Harvey Company mule wrangler, Robert Hinkle, was arguing with his wife, a hostess at El Tovar, in the crowded piano bar. An uninvolved tourist tried to intercede by saying "Hey, leave the woman alone." Hinkle reached under the table, pulled out a .357 magnum revolver and shot the Good Samaritan in the face at close range. After the single shot, patrons in the bar disarmed and subdued the wrangler. Hinkle was arrested and spent the next fifteen years in the Arizona State Penitentiary.

Could this be the ghost many of the bartenders see when they close the lounge late at night? One of the bartenders happened to glance up in the back bar mirror and watched a shadowy figure of a man walking across the room. He quickly turned around and there was not a soul in the lounge with him.

"This hotel has lots of ghosts," one of the waitresses said, tallying three occasions. "We have seen the old hanging lamps swaying, a presence of a woman standing on the staircase, and one of my co-workers tripped over what she felt was a leg in the hallway of the hotel. When she looked back, nobody was there."

El Tovar guests have seen ghostly shadows flitting about

near the downstairs rest rooms. Some have heard whispering voices, and toilets have been known to flush in what was thought to be empty stalls.

Parapsychologist Suzi Sebek has conducted ghost tours at El Tovar from time to time. Sebek believes one of the ghosts in the old hotel is Mary Colter, whose presence is felt in several buildings on the rim. Although Colter never spent the night in the Mary Colter Suite, the room at El Tovar is named in her honor just the same. A portrait painting of Mary Colter hangs in the room and visitors insist Colter's eyes seem to follow and watch their every move.

Be sure to take a few minutes to stroll through El Tovar lobby. The subdued lighting emits somewhat of an essence of the Addams Family parlor, with the mounted forest animals staring down at you from the rustic log cabin walls. With hundreds of suicides, murders, and accidental falling deaths in and near El Tovar, there is no doubt that a few of the guests who checked in to the hotel, have not yet checked out.

HOPI
HOUSE
HAUNTS

opi House, built in 1905, is a large multistory building of stone masonry, shaped and built like a traditional Hopi pueblo structure. It was originally planned to house the main salesrooms for Fred Harvey Indian Arts. Mary Colter designed the building, which sits directly across the courtyard from El Tovar. The building was constructed with the help of several Hopi workmen using local stone and wood. This was the first of several buildings architect Colter designed for Grand Canyon National Park. Colter's vision of the Hopi House was to be a living museum where Hopi Indians could reside and work, creating and selling traditional arts and crafts. Guests at El Tovar were encouraged to visit Hopi House to observe the Hopi artisans at their craft and purchase their goods.

The multiple roofs of the structure are set in various levels to give the impression of a pueblo in a Hopi village. The sandstone walls and brick are reddish in color. Small windows, like those of true Hopi buildings, let in just a trickle of sunlight. Construction on Hopi House was finished on January 1, 1905, just a few days before El Tovar was completed.

Inside, the rooms have ceilings of saplings, grasses, and twigs with a mud coating that rests on peeled log beams. There are corner fireplaces and small niches in the walls. The openings from one room to another are small, with wooden door frames made of peeled saplings. The first floor is used as a sales area.

The original stairwell that the public once climbed to reach the second story is decorated with Hopi sand paintings on each side of the adobe walls. These were painted by Fred Kabotie, the same artist who later did the artwork in Desert View Tower. The second story is now used as an art gallery sales area. One corner fireplace on the second floor is decorated with a "bulto" (Spanish religious statue) attached to the mantle.

Also on this floor is a room called "the kiva," which contains a Hopi shrine. Once, religious artifacts such as kachinas and bald eagle prayer feathers were housed here, along with other Hopi religious artifacts, *manos* and *metates* for grinding corn, pieces of pottery and baskets. The room included a beautiful Hopi sand painting and ceremonial altar. Access to this room was through a small handmade door.

The ceremonial room was used for about ninety years. It is one of the few kivas that exist outside of Hopi land. There was once a beautiful sand painting on the floor, covered with glass. Someone accidently stepped on the glass, which caused it to shatter. Crushed glass embedded into the rare piece of art. The Hopi elders came to the kiva and gathered up the remaining sand. They returned it to the depths of the Grand Canyon. The kiva was deconsecrated by the elders in 1998 by removing most of the sacred artifacts stored in the room and taking them back to Hopi land. The altar and some pottery dating back to the 1800s remain behind. Out of respect to the Hopi religion, the kiva door was locked and covered with a false wall.

The third floor provided housing for the manager of Hopi House. It was also used as a residence for some of the Hopi artists who worked in the building. It is presently the break room for Hopi House employees. The apartment has two bedrooms, a bath, living room/dining room, kitchen, and entrance hall.

Ken Merritt has worked at Hopi House for about five years and boasts a total of over seventeen years in the park. Merritt took us on a private tour of the historic building, giving us a lesson in its past and the lowdown on the Hopi House ghosts.

He led us up the center stairway that leads to the Hopi House fine art gallery. The gallery features fine pottery, jewelry and other Native American crafts that are for sale.

"Sometimes jewelry disappears for a day," he chuckled. "One of the ladies was up here checking in the jewelry and set a bracelet down on the counter near the register. When it was time to close for the evening, she noticed the bracelet was missing. She called me upstairs and we searched everywhere for it, but it was nowhere to be found. I told her not to worry...it will show up. Sure enough, the next morning we came upstairs to start a new search, and there was the bracelet lying on the counter right where she had originally put it!"

Another young man who worked in Hopi House has

found items moved around, inside the locked jewelry cases. The black-and-silver jewelry in one of the cases has been targeted the most often. The showcase items have fallen off the display stands or been found in complete disorder. He is baffled over the disturbances since he is the only employee with the key to the cases.

The same employee said he continuously sees what looks like the dried peas found in trail mix strewn across the floor each morning when he opens the shop. The floors are swept each evening as part of closing duties, but the mysterious dried peas often appear the next day. Ken Merritt noted he had seen the peas too. There is a no-food-or-drink policy in Hopi House so the chances of trail mix being spilled night after night would seem pretty low.

Merritt and others have seen, out of the corners of their eyes, the spirit of a man dressed in black standing near the second floor fireplace. Ken said the mysterious gentleman appears quite often, but never stays around for very long. The spirit quickly fades into the walls of the old pueblo as soon as he is discovered. No one knows who this man might be. Merritt suggested it could be one of the craftsmen that worked in Hopi House returning for a visit.

Merritt believes the activity on the floor is due to the hidden kiva, that ancient spirits are attracted to the reproduction worship site and still come and go from time to time. "There a few Grand Canyon ghosts known to haunt Hopi House," Merritt explained. "The 'Brown Boys' can be heard running around upstairs in the late evening. They have been known to turn off computers and throw merchandise on the floor if they don't like how it's arranged. They've even lined up kachina dolls in a row that were found in the morning by the surprised employees. In true poltergeist fashion, the 'Brown Boys' just make a general nuisance of themselves."

Merritt believes the prankster "Brown Boys" are a pair of young Hopi men who are rumored to have drowned in the Colorado River. He has seen the lights in the jewelry cases turned on and off by unseen hands, and watched as small rocks flew at him and hit the floor. He believes the "Brown Boys" mean no harm.

Ken Merritt took us up a back staircase that led to the apartment on the third floor. Our first stop was in its tiny kitchen.

"Check out the view," Merritt pointed to the window over the kitchen sink, "Can you imagine doing the dishes and enjoying this scenery?"

Glancing out the window, we saw that the majestic Grand Canyon was only yards away. Merritt led us through each room of the spacious apartment that was once the home of several Hopi artisans. We asked him about the paranormal activity that occurs on the third floor.

"The most common report is the sound of a woman's footsteps walking across the wooden floor," he explained. We believe it is a woman because we hear short, light-footed steps."

Merritt opened up a small door that led out to a rooftop patio. He chuckled when he told us the Travel Channel had come there to film the Travelocity gnome standing on the edge of the patio overlooking the canyon.

Back downstairs, Ken had a few theories of his own for the reasons why Hopi House is so haunted.

"The Hopis believe the Grand Canyon is the entrance to Hell. Ghosts that haunt the Hopi mesas come back to the canyon every day," he told us. "It gets quiet around here

when the spirits leave for the kachina dances in Hopi land...
but they always seem to return after a while."

Merritt has always wanted to set up surveillance cam-
eras throughout Hopi House to see just what happens in the
building after hours, and has invited the MVD Ghostchasers
paranormal team back to do an investigation sometime.

The ghosts of Hopi House are not to be feared. After all,
in the Hopi culture, everything is about peace and harmony.
Hopi House is located on the Rim Trail in Grand Canyon Village near El Tovar.

GRAND CANYON SITES WITH SPOOKY NAMES

S everal landmarks in the Grand Canyon hold names right out of a horror movie. Most of the sites are located deep in the canyon, but are very accessible if you are a hiker and don't mind a more physical means of hunting the Grand Canyon ghosts.

GHOST ROCK

The Ghost Rock Trail is a short but vigorous hike from the North Rim to the Esplanade, and continues on to an interesting archaeological site. The easy-to-navigate pathway follows Thunder River Trail to just above the Esplanade.

Ghost Rock has been used by mortal man for a long time. Ancient people drew large petroglyphs of two ghosts on the rocky overhang, giving the isolated location its name. Pot sherds and stone flakes have been found at the site, along with old tin cans and horseshoes from trail-riding cowboys seeking its shelter in days gone by.

From the Indian Hollow trailhead, the path crosses a wash and heads south following the canyon downstream. Soon the trail leaves the wash and climbs a ridge with a panoramic view of the Grand Canyon.

Leaving the overlook, the trail descends over a couple of short switchbacks, and then begins a long traverse to the west on top of Toroweap Cliffs.

Below the cliffs are a few more switchbacks, but the route to Ghost Rock goes straight down the slope. It runs around the east side of a red hill. On the south side of the red hill is a shelter with a tree for shade. From the rocky shelter, Ghost Rock is about one air mile southwest.

Ghost Rock is a huge red overhanging rock with life-size petroglyphs painted high on a forty-foot sandstone dome wall. The two wispy, white ghost characters are very eerie and mysterious looking. They are said to be ghosts of the ancient ancestors of the Native American tribes. South of the ghosts are other petroglyphs that show circles and interlocking semicircles. Just north of the ghost paintings is what seems to have been a large living area. There pieces of pottery and stone tools have been recovered.

Stay a spell and try your hand at communicating with the ghosts and the Native American people that inhabited the area before you. Perhaps they will guide you safely back to your vehicle.

PHANTOM ROCK

There are many speculations to how Phantom Ranch acquired its name. It is said to be named after Phantom Creek, which itself seems to be hidden away from view—like a phantom. Legend tells us that prospectors called it Phantom because of the eerie foggy mist that filled the air on cold mornings deep in the canyon. Perhaps it seemed like a ghostly phantom because the obscure oasis cannot be seen from the rim. It is mysteriously tucked away in the folds of the Phantom Fault. Others proclaim it was named after the ominous Phantom Rock, the landmark rock formation located about two miles north of Phantom Ranch along the North Kaibab Trail.

A hiker can see the Phantom Rock only for a few yards from the trail. It seems to lurk from behind the rocky landscape along the pathway. The tall, spooky rock formation resembles a dark-cloaked human figure in the distance.

SKELETON POINT

Skeleton Point is the focal spot of a six-mile round-trip hike on what has sometimes been nicknamed the "back bone of the Kaibab Trail." Although it does not go deep down into the Grand Canyon like the Bright Angel Trail, it offers a breathtaking view of the Colorado River from the scenic viewpoint.

This trail is also used less by backpackers and mule riders than Bright Angel, but is not for the faint-hearted hiker. There are narrow, steep switchbacks on what looks like a sheer cliff. A spiny-looking pathway resembling rib bones, hence the name "skeleton point," leads down to a comforting plateau.

Skeleton Point offers ghostly images of another kind.

Embedded in the aged flat sandstone are the skeletal fossil footprints of mammal-like reptiles and embedded imprints of spooky spiders.

This steep trail has no shade. It is advised to take lots of water with you on this hike. Avoid it during midday hours in the hot summer months in order to escape becoming a ghostly skeleton yourself.

HAUNTED CANYON

Haunted Canyon is one of the North Rim canyons east of Kaibab Trail. Its name is associated with nearby Haunted Creek. Some hikers say the canyon and creek were so named because their beauty will remain a haunting memory in your mind for as long as you live. Others say it is because of the many mysterious buttes and mesas lying deep down below in the bowels of the canyon.

This canyon is located past Phantom Ranch, where most hikers gather to rest or prepare for their return trip up the South Rim. Trails in the Haunted Canyon take you out to the backcountry known to serious hikers and true adventurers of the Grand Canyon. Haunted Canyon offers views of some mystical landmarks given the modern names of Manu Temple, Buddha Temple, Buddha Cloister, Cheops Pyramid, and Shiva Temple" There is lots of *experienced*-level hiking involved when exploring Phantom and Haunted Canyon.

COLORADO RIVER RUNNERS ALIVE & LONG-GONE

I spoke to a Colorado River runner who worked as a guide in the Grand Canyon for nearly thirty years. He has since moved on to a teaching career in the state of Hawaii. Kevin Johnson had to think for a while before he decided to tell his tale. Being a bit of a skeptic, he admitted he really didn't believe in ghosts. Then again, nothing paranormal ever happened to him—just those around him. This led him to believe there *is* something out there, but maybe he was just not as open to it.

Kevin's story took place about fifteen years ago when he was an active river guide for Arizona River Runner tours. It started out as "just another tour" with a group of people ready for action along the Colorado River. One of the rafters was a refined thirtyish lady from New York City. This married woman was a city girl through and through. He could see that she was struggling to keep up with the others. She was not accustomed to the harsh Arizona heat, and this was probably her first real camping trip. Sleeping and eating outdoors was a new adventure to her—let alone having to deal with no privy facilities. But she was a trouper. She didn't whine, complain, or demand special treatment. She hung in there with the rest of the rafters and Kevin respected that.

One evening, as the rafters called it a day, they pulled off to an area known in the Grand Canyon as the "bloody ledges." Kevin chuckled and explained that the guides nicknamed the area the "bloody ledges" because of ledged rocks that protrude at water level. Almost everyone stubs their toes on the ledges, and you find spots of blood here and there. It is located close to Mile 150, where Kanab Canyon comes in from the north. This area is known as Muav Gorge. It is quite narrow and there are no cool sandy beaches—only the hot rocky ledges where the sun beats down all day long.

The group fixed their dinner and talked about the wonderful scenery they had floated past earlier that day. With another full day of rafting ahead of them, they laid their sleeping bags over the hot ledges and prepared to sleep. Kevin recalled it as a typically oven-hot midsummer evening, with a full moon and lots of stars in the sky.

The next morning Kevin was one of the first to rise, and he started making the coffee for his group. The aroma began to arouse the others from their sleep, including the gal from New York. She sat up, and remained seated on her sleeping bag for quite some time. She had a puzzled look on her face as she glanced among her tour companions. It was as though she was trying to make sense of something troubling her.

"Who were those guys last night?" she finally asked.

"What guys?" Kevin handed her a cup of coffee.

"Those guys who came to the camp in the middle of the night...didn't you see them?"

The group looked at each other and shrugged their shoulders—apparently they all slept like babies and didn't hear a thing. The frustrated woman looked over to the water's edge and glanced up the river as though she expected to see someone.

"Just what did you see?" Kevin asked. She had everybody's attention now.

"Well," she rubbed the sleep from her eyes, "I had a really hard time sleeping last night—between the heat and the rocky mattress—so I sat up for a while just listening to the water, and the rest of you snoring...all of a sudden a wooden boat pulled up to where we are camped. None of you heard the wooden boat clunking against the rocks?"

Everyone in the rafting party looked at each other, and shook their heads "no."

"Then," she continued, "three men got out of the boat. They looked out of place because they were wearing overalls—like farmers wear. They had on long-sleeved shirts and boots! They wore hats and all three of them had beards. I could see them clearly because the moon was so bright."

The woman sat down on the rocks and still seemed a bit confused.

"The three men turned around and looked over at me, and I began to feel a bit uneasy. You were all asleep. One of the men started walking towards me and I blurted out 'What do you need? You need to talk to our guide, Kevin!' I was hoping one of you would wake up to talk to this guy."

By now the group was mesmerized by her story, "So, where did they go?"

"The man never spoke a word," she reported. "He just turned around and got back in the wooden boat with the two men and headed down the river."

"Wooden boat...?" Kevin asked, "not the type of a craft we are using?"

"No, she nodded, "wooden boat—sort of looked like those old fashion irons the pioneer ladies had to use. You know...the kind you had to heat up on the stove."

Kevin grinned. He knew exactly what kind of boat she was talking about. The early river explorers and rafters use to make their way down the Colorado in wooden boats called "cataract boats." Being a city girl, the woman had no clue what the early Wild West rafters used as boats for traveling the Colorado rapids. He knew there was no modern river rafting company on the Colorado using the old fashioned sailing vessels and, besides, the river runners always know *who* is on the river. Kevin said he never saw the ghostly men in the cataract boat on the river again...but never forgot the moonlit night when two veils crossed over into one for just a short moment in time.

A group of college students on a month-long canyon trip had their own encounter as they camped one evening. They were all settled near Blacktail Canyon for the night. If you hike up the narrow, side canyon in silence, the walls seem to close in and surround you. The walls are plum-colored Tapeats sandstone. They curve over your head, and only a thin strip of the sky peeks out above you. It is so still that one hears every drop falling into the pools of water scattered along the ground. Every bird singing, every thunderclap, and any musical note seems to echo from the walls.

It had been raining when the group finished dinner and

the students eventually moved to their tents pitched among the rocks and boulders. The guides knew of a deep overhanging ledge of sandstone near the canyon entrance where they could lay out the bags and sleep untouched by the falling rain. It was very dark at the mouth of the canyon and, without a flashlight, one could be in danger.

One of the guides began to hear the sound of someone hitting a drum. He listened intensely for a few minutes. He decided it was only the beating rapids and lay back down to get some sleep. Then an old Indian man came to him, holding a stone knife. The rafting guide described the elder as having white hair and wearing something around his neck. The guide couldn't really make out the features of the elder's face. The old man did not say a word. Somehow the guide felt the mysterious man wanted to show him something— something bad. He felt death, but not his own. He thought he should leave—that he was not supposed to be there! He believed the old man was telling him "they" wanted this group out of there. The mystifying elder spoke no words. The guide was so scared that he became paralyzed in the darkness. He could not move. Was this really happening, or was it just a dream?

He turned to his partner and asked if he was still awake. Indeed, he was. Both of the outdoorsmen confirmed they had had the same terrible nightmare, shared the same feeling of dread about camping here, and agreed they better roll up and get out of there. They gathered up their sleeping bags and dashed out into the rain to set up a tent near the sleeping students. Then, suddenly, the drumming sounds ceased.

The rafter has returned to Blacktail Canyon several times after that evening, but he swears he will never try to sleep under the ledge at night again. He's camped near the same site, but only on the debris fan. He even tried sitting under the overhang, but has never heard the drumming again.

THE
LEGEND OF
BERT LOPER

*B*ert Loper has become a part of Grand Canyon folklore as a ghostly apparition rowing a phantom boat in the dark waters of the Colorado River. His spirit has been known to prowl through the camps, playing pranks on the tired river runners and guests.

In *Tales from the Grand Canyon* (Edna Evans, 1985), it states that Albert (Bert) Loper was driven by the powerful Colorado River. It seems to be a feeling that can overtake a person and make him emotionally spellbound by the sounds and beauty of the canyon walls. By 1907, Loper was prospecting and river running along the Colorado. He worked the river scene for fifty years before his demise. Sometimes he guided his boat through the canyon successfully, and sometimes the boat was wrecked or destroyed so he could not finish the run. Bert would not give up. He made his repairs or returned to the river with a new craft. By 1939 he was listed among the first five hundred men to successfully run the Colorado River in the Canyon.

Bert worked as a guide or chief boatman for scientific expeditions. His experience gave him valuable knowledge of the canyons and rapids of the Colorado River. He was always willing to share his notes, advice, and recommendations to the other river runners. This made him a well respected leader of the runners, and he was given the nickname of "Grand Old Man of the Colorado."

As the outdoorsman aged, ill heath due to a bad gall bladder began to slow him down just a little. Bert was stubborn, and determined to spend his eightieth birthday on a trip down the Colorado. He spent the winter of 1948-1949 building a special plywood boat for his upcoming summer excursion. He named his new boat the *Grand Canyon*.

His birthday was July 31. On July 7, 1949, he launched from Lee's Ferry for his birthday voyage. He brought along a passenger, Wayne Nichol, two unmanned boats, and a rubberized raft carrying rations and supplies. The very next day, at Mile 24.5, the *Grand Canyon* capsized. Nichol was able to swim to shore, but Bert was last seen floating with the current ahead of his overturned boat. It is not known if he drowned or had a heart attack.

The next day his boat was found lodged on a rocky ledge near mile marker 41.5. His friends hauled the boat high upon the shoreline and left it at the site. On the front deck they painted his epitaph:

Bert Loper
The Grand Old Man of the Colorado
Born July 31, 1869   Died July 8, 1949

Near mile 25

No trace of Bert was found. Years passed and his battered boat remained on the shore continuing to weather in the elements. Twenty-five years later, DNA confirmed it was Loper's skeletal remains that were discovered near Cardenas Creek. He was buried with his wife in Sandy, Utah.

Tales of Bert's adventures on the river live on, and some of the river runners have turned his stories into folklore—making him a Grand Canyon legend. They say Bert's ghost still roams the Colorado. The river rafters believe Bert is angry with the increasing travel on his river, and the disrespect the river is occasionally shown. His ghost haunts camping areas along the Colorado and has been credited as the cause of all the trivial annoyances that occur on rafting trips.

The guides have come to associate Bert with the playful ghostly pranks that happen on the river trips. If the coffee pot or water jug tips over for no reason, or the camping or rafting equipment disappears from sight, it is always explained as "Bert Loper's ghost did it."

Listen carefully at night. Sometimes, above the roar of the river you can hear a ghostly noise. In the distance you will hear the creaking and thumping sound of old wooden oars against the metal oarlocks. Bert Loper is out there...rowing the Grand Canyon, harassing the rafters and snatching their equipment in the darkness of the night. Some say "Bert Loper has become the Davey Jones of the mighty Colorado River."

THE HYDES: HAUNTING HONEYMOONERS

Glen and Bessie Hyde, a young, newlywed couple from Idaho, decided to spend their honeymoon rafting down the Colorado River in the autumn of 1928.

Glen was a tall, slender, yet athletic man of twenty-eight, and Bessie was a petite ninety-pound woman twenty-two years old. Photographs of the couple standing together show that Bessie barely came to her husband's shoulder. The rafting adventure was most likely his idea. Bessie, not quite the outdoors enthusiast her husband was, went along with the plan because it would make her famous as the first woman known to raft the entire Colorado River.

The Hydes built their boat in Green River, Utah. It was an open, blunt ended scow, and measured twenty feet long, five feet wide, and three feet deep—with a sweeping oar at each end. It was a cumbersome-looking craft compared to other decked or rowboat scows used by the river runners.

They launched from Green River on October 20, 1928, and reached Bright Angel Creek twenty-six days later. Leaving their scow secure and tied to the river bank, they hiked up the newly constructed South Kaibab Trail and the seven miles to the South Rim for supplies and a good night's sleep.

While in Grand Canyon Village, they ran into Emery Kolb. Kolb was shocked to learn that the Hydes were not wearing life preservers on the river and offered them the use of some of his. Glen Hyde smiled and turned down the offer. He assured Emery that he and Bessie were both good swimmers and the life preservers would not be necessary. Emery knew from experience that dangerous waters were just ahead, and was deeply concerned about their safety.

Emery could not help noticing a sort of haunted look in Bessie's eyes. She did not seem very eager to continue on the excursion. The harshness of river life was starting to take a toll on her and she was all but ready to head for home. She admitted that Glen had been thrown into the river twice and she had barely managed to get a rope out to him. In spite of Bessie's worries, Glen insisted that they must continue this once-in-a-lifetime adventure.

During the couple's visit, Kolb's daughter, Edith came out of the studio to meet the special guests. Edith, who was not much younger than Bessie, was very neatly groomed and dressed in the latest fashion. Bessie glanced down at her own worn, slightly soiled attire, and yearned for the raft trip to be over. Looking at the dainty polished shoes on Kolb's daughter, Bessie sighed, "I wonder if I shall ever wear pretty shoes again."

The next day, Emery Kolb photographed the Hydes standing near the rim of the canyon. They assured him they would be back to pick up the photo after they completed their trip.

The couple hiked back down the trail to a small tourist camp. A wealthy traveler asked if he could travel down the Colorado with them for a day. They agreed and allowed their passenger to ride as far as Hermit Camp. On November 18, 1928, the passenger photographed the couple near the water with their scow.

After that day, the honeymooners were never seen again. It was as though they vanished off the face of the Earth.

The Kolbs could not get the young couple off their minds and didn't get much sleep for the next few nights. Both Emery and Edith were haunted by Bessie's parting words.

When the couple did not reach the end of their trip in Needles according to their schedule, Hyde's father organized a search party. An army plane from March Air Base was sent in to help. It was the first plane to venture into the inner gorge of the Grand Canyon. The pilot spotted the scow about fourteen miles below the mouth of Diamond Creek. Ellsworth Kolb arrived from California to aid with the search and rescue efforts.

They reached the Hydes' scow on December 1, 1928. It was floating upright with about fourteen inches of water in the bottom. Both oars were in place and the dragging rope was tangled among the rocks in deep water. Glen's gun was there, along with Bessie's diary, camera, and notebook. Ellsworth's book, *Through the Grand Canyon*, which the couple had been using as a guide, was open on the seat undisturbed.

A search along the shore located the couple's tracks about seven miles about Diamond Creek. Farther down the shore, Glen's foot print was found along the rapids. The tracks led to the river, but did not return to the shoreline.

What happened to the honeymooners remains a mystery. Emery Kolb had a theory based on what he knew of the couple's usual plan of action. Bessie would stand on the river bank holding the scow's rope while Glen walked ahead a distance to examine the next rapid. It is possible she had been pulled or blown into the river current, and Glen jumped in to save her, and the Colorado River claimed both their lives. The rapids at Mile 232 are very difficult and that may have been where the terrible accident occurred. The scow floated on for another five miles until the trailing rope was caught on the rocks.

Only the spirits of the Colorado River know what really happened to the young Idaho couple doomed never to finish their honeymoon trip. The river guides often tell their rafting parties the tale of the Hydes. They all agreed the disappearance of the couple is one of the canyon's most enduring mysteries, and keep a vigilant eye out for their ghosts. It may always remain as one of the Canyon's ghostly secrets—as neither Hyde nor hair was ever found.

GRAND CANYON'S "EGYPTIAN" MUMMIES

In 1908, G.E. Kinkaid, a veteran of thirty years of service with the Smithsonian Institution, found the entrance of a mysterious underground citadel at the base of the Grand Canyon. It was here, they say, that he made an amazing discovery.

Climbing up the sheer walls in what is known as Marble Canyon, Kinkaid found himself in a huge chamber hewn of solid rock. Upon entering the enormous cave, he was surrounded by mummies as well as a shrine. Everywhere he looked there were passageways that led to more caverns. It was somewhat like a scene from an Indiana Jones adventure.

These caverns were said to house weapons, vases, and even mummies of Egyptian origin. Kinkaid's story appeared in the April 5, 1909, issue of the *Arizona Gazette* newspaper. There was an additional story that a Professor Jordon was also at the investigation site. The pair claimed they also had located a shrine in the cavern that resembled the cross-legged figure of Buddha. The face of the statue looked Asian and each of its hands held a "lily."

The crypt contained tiers of mummies with, at their feet, copper cups and swords. They looked as though they were barracks of ancient warriors. One explorer said the passageways smelled "snaky" and they gave him an uneasy feeling of heavy gloom.

The story was later declared by the Smithsonian to be a fake and the museum denied that any Egyptian artifacts were found in the Americas, let alone in the Grand Canyon. Many of the canyon's buttes and mesas had been named after the deities of Egyptian and India, stemming from the early explorers' love of ancient archaeology. Landmarks in the Grand Canyon were dubbed Cheops Pyramid, Tower of Ra (both Egyptian references), Shiva Temple (India), and Manu Temple (India). Fortunately, the caves of the Grand Canyon do not come with a curse such as that claimed for the pharaoh Tutankhamen's tomb.

Some historians believe what may have been discovered was the "Sipapu" or the Hopi underworld or ceremonial chamber. The Hopi believe the Sipapu is the gateway through which the souls of mankind emerged from the underworld. Hopi legend suggests that the previous world had been destroyed by a great flood. Spider Grandmother, a Hopi goddess, sealed the righteous into hollow reeds, saving them from destruction. These ancient ancestors then floated for a long time and used islands as stepping stones. When they reached a mountainous wall, the ancient ancestors climbed up into a new world...from a hole inside the Grand Canyon.

The Hopi believe the dead also can use the portal to come back.

Chuar and Temple buttes near the confluence of the Colorado and Little Colorado rivers was the site of the deadly in-air crash of United Airlines Flight 781 and TWA Flight 2 over Grand Canyon in 1956. The small ravine between the two buttes became known as Crash Canyon. Grand Canyon ranger K.J. Glover told *Haunted Hikes* author Andrea Lankford about an experience she had when hiking in the Sipapu area. She believes she saw airline passengers walking along a trail near the crash site fifty years after the accident. She had camped between Chuar and Temple buttes after a long day of hiking. Suddenly, she heard voices outside her tent. She peeked out the flap only to see about a dozen or more people walking up the trail. They were dressed in city clothes—the traveling clothes of the 1950s, button-up dress shirts, ties on the men, and below-the-knee dresses on the women. They were having conversations with each other as though nothing was unusual. Following closely behind them were five or six Native Americans. They spoke in a language Lankford could not understand. When she climbed out of her tent to look around and see where they were headed, the group vanished. Could it have been the ancient Hopis leading the deceased passengers to the secret world of the Sipapu?

Officials were able to identify only a few of the victims. The remains of the rest of the passengers were buried in a mass grave in Grand Canyon Pioneer Cemetery and Citizens Cemetery in Flagstaff, Arizona.

The National Park Service at Grand Canyon has labeled this area dangerous for inexperienced hikers, because of the hazardous bottomless caves within the canyon walls. Native Americans are superstitious about the area, as are many canyon park rangers. Some pilots refuse to look down when they fly overhead. Several hikers near the area have felt nauseous or sick—and some have been struck by lightning. Maybe it is best that the hidden tombs are eternally left alone.

UFOS
VISITING THE
GRAND CANYON

A few years back, a team of UFO experts was summoned to examine strange debris found at the bottom of the Grand Canyon. It was said they discovered the wreckage of a UFO that crashed over 4,000 years ago. Scientists inspected the UFO and found it to be in fairly good condition despite the crash landing and the alleged age of the craft.

The spaceship was made of unknown metallic material and still emitted low levels of radiation. It measured about 50 feet across at its widest point and was 102 feet long. The wreckage was removed from the site and taken to a secluded, *secret* location. It was reported that the craft could easily carry a crew of twelve to twenty passengers. Carbon dating showed the crash occurred at the base of the Grand Canyon around 2000 B.C.

The UFO was recovered in limestone rubble not far from an area called Comanche Point near the Colorado River. Scientists believed the surviving crew lived near the crash site for several years after it hurtled to the Earth. Numerous Indian paintings found in nearby caves show strange human-looking creatures with bulbous heads. Some researchers believe these creatures could be the same aliens who arrived with the ancient UFO.

Many paranormal investigators believe that ghosts and UFO aliens are one and the same. Some people have experienced dreams where they were told through the help of spirits that their long-dead loved ones live on a distant planet. Both ghosts and UFO aliens have related stories of lost civilizations. Both are tied to out-of-body experiences. Ghost sightings are considered as a sign or a possible side effect of alien contact or abduction. It would not be an odd occurrence to witness a UFO in the canyon.

You will find numerous pieces of film footage on the Internet of supposed UFOs darting in and out of the canyon walls, photographed by Grand Canyon visitors year after year. Some were staged hoaxes, while others innocently mistook a hovering helicopter for a UFO. Other visitors have witnessed mysterious lights flitting in the canyon skies on star-filled evenings.

I spoke to one of the canyon river runners who had his own close encounter with an UFO in Grand Canyon back in 1985. James Henrick was leading a river run with a group of tired rafters who had pulled along the banks to set up camp for the night. It was just dusk when the group noticed a low object hovering over the Colorado River not far from their campsite.

"It stayed in one place and hovered over the water," James stated. "I remember it had red and bluish lights."

The river rafters stopped what they were doing and stared downriver. As they watched, the silent UFO occasionally tipped at a very slight angle.

James reported that there were no exhaust, no sound, and no vapors. "It was very eerie and I will never forget the experience," he said. "It must have stayed in that one spot over the river for about ten minutes. I remember some of the river rafters were starting to feel a bit uneasy—or even frightened."

Then, he said it rose straight into the sky and disappeared. The group was pretty quiet the rest of the night and none of them could take their eyes off the sky above them. The next morning, around the breakfast campfire, the group reconfirmed what they had witnessed.

The Grand Canyon just could be the exploration destination of space aliens who study our planet from afar and wonder just what that huge gash in the planet might be. These visitors could be on missions to photograph and explore the Grand Canyon, so give a welcoming smile when you look up into the sky on a starlit night.

THE PHANTOM
OF THE
CANYON

$\mathbf{P}$hantom Ranch was built on a site once inhabited by Native Americans. Ruins of pit houses and a ceremonial kiva were found in and around the grounds. Fred Harvey had been commissioned to build a tourist haven at the bottom of the Grand Canyon, so once again he employed the talents of designer Mary Colter. Colter liked to add a bit of spirit to her designs, and agreed on the name "Phantom Ranch because of the supernatural or distant echoes she heard at nearby" Phantom Creek. The name evoked romantic images of ghouls and ghosts.

All of the building material, except for the rocks, had to be hauled in by mule train. Phantom Ranch was completed by 1922 at a price of a quarter of a million dollars. The relatively high cost, for those days, was partly because the facility was complete with modern, indoor bathrooms.

Tucked in along Bright Angel Creek on the north side of the Colorado River, Phantom Ranch can be reached only by mule, on foot, or by river raft. The rustic cabins and main lodge are built of wood and native stone. The ranch has been described as an oasis in the desert, with its cabins protected by shade trees dotted along Phantom Creek.

There is much speculation to why the word *Phantom* became associated with the area. Phantom Ranch is said to be named after Phantom Creek, which appears to be hidden from view—like a phantom. Legend tells us that prospectors called it Phantom because of the eerie mist filling the air on cold mornings deep in the canyon. Perhaps it seemed like a ghost because the elusive oasis, tucked away in the folds of the Phantom Fault, cannot be seen from the rim. Others proclaim it is named after the ominous Phantom Rock. This formation sits about two miles north of the ranch along North Kaibab Trail. It is a rocky projection that sits along the trail and resembles a dark-cloaked, phantom-like figure.

One of the mule-guides told me the old bunkhouse at Phantom Ranch is known to be haunted. A female guide was startled when she saw the ghost of a former mule packer who had died of natural causes standing inside the bunkhouse.

"I bet that was creepy," I raised an eyebrow.

"Not as creepy as sleeping in the same bed he died in," the mule guide chuckled.

Ranger Scott Kraynak was on his way home for lunch when we pulled him aside to chat near the Bright Angel Trail and Kolb Studio. We asked if he had heard any ghost stories from hikers, or seen any unexplained events along the trails.

Ranger Scott has sat and talked with many of the hikers and campers near Phantom Ranch on his daily trail walks. He reported that the most common occurrence hikers, campers, and rafters experience near Phantom Ranch is the feeling of unseen souls passing by in the darkness at night. These ghostly hikers could be unfortunate backpackers who died on the trail because of accidents, medical emergencies, or dehydration. Hikers or campers sitting along the trail often report seeing dark shadows of what looks like people walking past them. Sometimes they are puzzled by the sound of footsteps as invisible backpackers shuffle by. Other hikers have seen mysterious energy balls of light called "ghost lights" flickering along the trail.

The ghost of Rees B. Griffiths, a former worker on the trail crew, still haunts the site of his demise. Griffiths was the trail foreman working with a team building the Kaibab trail deep in the canyon. On February 6, 1922, he and his crew were removing large rocks near the proposed site of the suspension bridge over the Colorado River. The workmen set off large amounts of dynamite in the rocky terrain.

After the blast, Griffiths climbed to the top of the rocks to inspect the excavation first hand. A huge boulder loosened by the explosions rolled down and carried him to the rocks below. Griffiths' body was crushed. He died about six hours later near Phantom Ranch. The man's last wish to his crew was to be buried in the Grand Canyon.

The rangers and the trail crew gave him the proper burial he requested. His grave is located north of the Colorado River between Phantom Ranch and the suspension bridge known as Black Bridge—just across from the pueblo ruins. It is in an alcove off the trail, right before the turnoff to the boat beach. A memorial plaque near the Kaibab Suspension Bridge reads:

Rees B Griffths
Trail foreman, National Park Service
Born October 10, 1873   Died February 6, 1922
In Grand Canyon he loves so well, as a result of injuries
received near this spot while in the performance
of his duty in building of Kaibab Trail

Griffiths has been seen by trail maintenance crews, hikers, and people camping nearby. He appears as a glowing light along the trail, a light that sometimes hovers over his grave. The small translucent ball of bluish light keeps a quiet vigil through the night.

Keep your eyes peeled for Phantom Rock. You will catch only a glimpse of it for a few hundred feet. Ghosts, phantoms...this hiking adventure could easily turn into a supernatural experience.

THE RED GARTER'S LADIES OF THE EVENING & THEIR CALLERS

The two-story building that houses the Red Garter Bed
and Bakery was built by a German tailor named August
Tetzlaff. It was constructed in 1897 in downtown Williams,
Arizona—the southern gateway city to the Grand Canyon.
The original keystone, with Tetzlaff's name and the comple-
tion date, is still above the arched entrance to the building.
Tetzlaff's establishment on "Saloon Row" was designed to
accommodate the needs of the cowboys, loggers, and railroad men who worked and settled near town. The building
boasted a saloon on the ground floor and a very popular bordello upstairs. The ladies were often seen hanging out of the
windows, calling out to the gentlemen who were arriving
on the trains or passing on the street. A doorway on the side
led to a steep flight of stairs since nicknamed "the Cowboy's

Endurance Test." The girls would listen for boot steps, and the madam greeted the callers at the top of the stairs and completed the financial transactions.

Longino Mora operated the downstairs saloon for several years. He sold bootlegged liquor goods out the back door during Prohibition, and prospered greatly. The front of the establishment was still a gathering point, but the bar and gaming tables were hidden away by a partition. Mr. Mora stated he had been married five times and fathered twenty five-children. His last wife, Clara, bore his last child when he was eighty years old. In his later years, Mora's health began to decline, and he eventually committed suicide by stabbing himself with a knife. He was ninety years old that year of 1938. He is buried in the Williams Cemetery.

Arizona Territory began to enforce the laws banning prostitution and gambling in 1907. But, local ordinances were usually passed to regulate where brothels could operate. The girls were licensed and taxed and made to take frequent medical exams. The saloons and brothels of Williams continued to flourish through the 1930s and 1940s. During World War II, when many men were called away to war, the brothels began to close down.

Legend states that a tragic murder took place on the stairs of the bordello in the early 1900s. A prostitute stabbed one of her customers in the back and he tumbled down the steep staircase. The force of the fall threw the man out the door at the bottom of the steps. The dead man lay on the sidewalk, horrifying passing pedestrians. Some guests believe the heavy boot steps they hear on the steps and hallways belong to the dead man's ghost.

The contemporary owner of the Red Garter, John Holst, bought the abandoned building in 1979 and began the painstaking task of renovating the former bordello into a first class bed-and-breakfast. In his research, Holst learned the B&B has operated as a Chinese restaurant, opium den, general store and boarding house. Traces of the Chinese operations were found in the back lot when older structures were torn down and removed. Holst changed the eight upstairs rooms—one belonging to the madam and seven for the "girls"—into four larger rooms complete with full baths. His dedicated work has given the Red Garter the honor of being placed on the National Register of Historic Places. The B&B has been in full operation since 1998.

As John Holst began his extensive reconstruction on the aged building, he was able to recognize every little creak and squeak within the walls. Late at night, usually around 11:30, he would hear a loud "CLUNK," which he described as a heavy door being slammed shut tight. Calling himself a "hard-core skeptic" about ghosts and the paranormal, Holst found himself popping out of his bed to make a nightly security walk through the darkened hallways and ground floor. He would always find the doors secured and locked.

Right from Holst's opening day, guests started reporting seeing a ghost of a young Hispanic woman with long hair in the room now named "Best Gal's Room." This particular room has windows that overlook the street below. When the bordello was in operation, the rooms in the back of the building were smaller and occupied by the newer or the less popular girls. The madam had her room in the center, near the parlor entry at the top of the stairs. The most popular ladies had the larger rooms with window views. They used these windows to attract and draw in clients.

Puzzled guests in the Best Gal's Room have encountered the ghostly young woman seeming to be alone and distraught in the middle of the night. The ghost has been given the name "Eve" and has beautiful, flowing black hair and dark eyes. She wears a long white gown and seems to be clutching in her hands an object that resembles a pill-box. The distressed spirit has been seen pacing the floor near the foot of the bed in the Best Gal's Room as though she is contemplating a life-changing decision. Guests say the spirit suddenly fades away and leaves them to ponder whether they were merely dreaming.

A photo has been discovered, one that shows Longino Mora and a couple of his children standing in the saloon in about 1934. The bar and poker tables were hidden behind the divider due to Prohibition laws. There is a young lady, presumably Eve, with long dark hair behind the counter and standing in front of a large mirror that does not reflect her image. Several paranormal teams have studied the photo to measure the distances and tried to prove or debunk the picture. They believe the photograph displays evidence of paranormal phenomena.

Visitors to the four hotel rooms in the Red Garter also report playful ghosts who bounce on or shake the mattresses, or seeing a slight impression of someone sitting on the edge of the bed. Many guests have been gently touched on the arm. Some have felt their hair being stroked, and one paranormal investigator said he felt someone tickling his mustache. A glimpse of a gentleman or cowboy is seen from time to time. Could it be one of the roving cowboys coming upstairs for a visit, or is it the spirit of Mr. Mora making sure all is well in his old establishment? This could explain the footsteps heard on the empty staircase and the hallway, and the jiggling of doorknobs.

Upon checking into the Best Gal's Room, we were prepared for a late-night visit from the mournful Eve. We placed "trigger items" such as perfume, lace gloves, and a shot of whisky on the bedside table to lure Eve into making her presence known.

Although there was no sign of the dark-haired specter, we did have a visit from a strong male energy. Our recording device picked up on the sound of heavy boot steps coming up the stairs and walking across the wooden floor, although no male guests were staying in the hotel that evening. Amazingly, we also detected the odor of a man's perspiration accompanied with stale whisky. Shadowy figures played hide and seek in the hallways. It was as though the girls were still dashing from room to room preparing to serve their special customers.

The Red Garter B&B is once again a popular resting spot for weary travelers who venture back and forth to the Grand Canyon on the trains leaving Williams for the South Rim each day. As you drive into town, you can't help but smile when you glance up to see the lovely mannequin dressed as a soiled dove waving her feathered boa to the passing traffic. The Red Garter offers guests a different sort of persuasion these days. Try one of the wonderful pastries created on the ground floor bakery. Each morning, the Red Garter Bakery conjures them up along with fruit and gourmet coffee for guests, residents and visitor. They may be sinfully delicious, but you know they will completely fulfill your wants and needs.

Red Garter Bed and Bakery
137 W Railroad Avenue
Williams, AZ 86046
928-635-1484; www.redgarter.com

CANYON MOTEL'S WANDERING CONDUCTOR

The town of Williams, Arizona, known as "Gateway to the Grand Canyon," was once a busy metropolis along the old Route 66 highway. Now, thanks to the popular Grand Canyon Railway Depot, it is flourishing with tourists once again. One of the original rustic motor lodges from the 1940s, the Canyon Motel, holds a ghost or two from those bygone "Mother Road" days.

Williams was a major hub for railroads in the late 1800s and early 1900s. Because this was an old railroad community, the owners of the Canyon Motel decided to move a couple of original 1928 cabooses onto their property and renovate them into unique lodging suites. They also brought in a Pullman rail car and made it into lodging as well. All of the train cars are equipped with baths, heaters, air conditioning, small refrigerators and microwaves, as well as cable television.

These unusual train car accommodations are frequently requested by travelers looking for somewhere out of the ordinary to rest their heads. Many of the guests have observed strange phenomena during their overnight caboose visits. Visitors have reported unexplained sounds during the night, lights flickering on and off for no apparent reason, and a few surprised tourists have seen an old conductor walking through the caboose swinging his dimly lit lantern in the darkened rail car.

One of the housekeepers stated that sometimes she has heard whispering or talking during the day while she worked. She described the chatter as sounding like a distant radio frequency. She knows there is nobody else around, but it catches her off guard just the same.

The Canyon Motel's hosts welcome ghost hunters who wish to spend the night. They hope that someone will capture paranormal activity on film or recording devices and open an ongoing investigation. Perhaps one of the guests will be able to debunk the myth of the conductor's wandering ghost, or maybe they can develop further proof that his residual visits actually exist.

The cabooses and rustic rooms can be reserved for your next adventure when you visit Williams. Whether you're riding the train to the Grand Canyon, or heading back home, you won't want to miss this travel experience.

The Canyon Motel & RV Park
1900 E. Rodeo Road, Rt 66
Williams, AZ 86048
928-635-4138; www.thecanyonmotel.com

GHOSTLY HARVEY GIRL AT WILLIAMS' TRAIN DEPOT

Fray Marcos, Fred Harvey's first eatery in Williams, Arizona, opened its doors in 1894 when the company took over a restaurant that had been in operation for about ten years. Architect Francis W. Wilson designed the Harvey company's next hotel and restaurant, which opened March 10, 1908. It was named to honor the Spanish Franciscan missionary Fray Marcos de Niza—the first European explorer of Arizona and New Mexico. This facility served as the southern depot for the Grand Canyon Railway, and took care of east-west mainline traffic along the Santa Fe Railroad until 1954.

The Fray Marcos offered twenty-two guest rooms and ten Harvey Girl dorm rooms for waitresses when it opened in 1908. In the 1920s, Harvey Company added a two-story addition with twenty-one new guest rooms. Travelers often stayed at the Fray Marcos while en route to the Grand Canyon by train or car. A sixty-three-mile spur line to the South Rim had gone into operation on September 17, 1901. A maintained automobile road was completed after the Grand Canyon was designated as a national park in 1919.

Many of the adventurous women who applied to be Harvey Girls sought this career opportunity as a way to meet eligible men of the West. They also knew it was possible to save for their trousseaux, education, and nest eggs. Several of the girls worked to help financially strapped families left behind in rural communities where employment for women was limited. Some came to escape abusive relationships back home, or to forget the past and start new lives. Many wanted to travel and see the world...or at least parts of this country they would have never experienced otherwise.

The women who were selected to be Harvey Girls were proud of their careers. The Harvey Girls were known by their professional attire and appearance. The original uniform consisted of a black ankle-length, long-sleeved dress with a white starched apron. The uniform was highlighted by a white collar with a black bow. Their hair was piled high and adorned with a bow headpiece. Black shoes and stockings completed their ensembles.

The staff of the Fray Marcos lived above the kitchen, on the second floor of the west wing. Each Harvey Girl shared a small, comfortable room with another. They did not have much space to spare in the double room. The work schedules kept them pretty busy, and when they were off duty, there were strict chaperones to deal with. Even with a 10:00 P.M. curfew, many of the girls managed to meet their admirers and future husbands, and invented ways to divert the chaperones. On their days off, the girls made use of railway passes to visit the Grand Canyon and other Arizona cities. They visited friends and traveled the vast lands of Northern Arizona in automobiles.

The Harvey Girls at the Fray Marcos kept the lunch room counter and dining room tables spotless and ready for the next train arrival at all times. When not serving hungry travelers, they polished the silver, cleaned the sparkling glasses, and kept the famous Fred Harvey coffee brewing. It was a busy job, but most of the girls renewed their contracts when they completed their six-month agreements.

Today, the building that housed the Fray Marcos depot restaurant and hotel is the Grand Canyon Railway ticket counter, museum and gift shop. The building has been returned to its original color scheme, and interior furnishings offer a vintage look. The fireplace that was once part of the lobby and dining area is now the centerpiece of the gift shop. The building is the largest and oldest poured concrete structure in the state of Arizona and holds a place on the National Register of Historic Places. The rooms where tired travelers slept are now used for offices and storage. But it seems that one of the Harvey Girls is still on duty at the old Harvey House, and many of the employees have witnessed her presence.

"We call her Clara," the pleasant cashier in the gift shop smiled. "I have not seen her myself, but I have felt her presence in the late afternoon or early evening when nobody else is in the shop. You can see something move out of the corner of your eye—or hear a movement from the back of the room, and then you just nod and acknowledge Clara. We feel Clara senses we are getting ready to close shop for the night and she is just tidying up the old Harvey House too."

The gift shop staff has noticed items tumbling to the floor such as books, hats, and souvenir T-shirts. All the items were properly displayed just moments before, so it seemed as if the ghost was just up to some fun and games. Sometimes the cashiers hear light footsteps of a woman's shoes clicking along the original tile floors as they count out the end-of-day receipts. Looking up, and expecting to see a customer—or a fellow employee, they are stunned to find the building completely empty.

The ticket counter area is another active areas of the depot. One staff member saw the spirit of a young woman lingering near the doorway. The vision of the smiling ghost lasted a few seconds and then she faded away. The counter clerk described the ghost as resembling a Harvey Girl dressed in a uniform like one she had seen in the museum's photograph collection.

Maintenance employees hesitate before going up the staircase to the second floor, where the Grand Canyon Railway offices are located. The second floor also is used for office and maintenance-supply storage. Several startled staff members have seen the black and white uniformed ghost of Harvey Girl Clara standing near the top of the second floor stairway. They refuse to go upstairs alone. Perhaps Clara's ghost is merely dashing downstairs from her dormitory room to greet the next breakfast train when she accidently bumps into the unsuspecting maintenance crew.

"My mother is good friends with one of the retired Harvey Girls who still resides in Williams," the cashier recalled as she rang up another customer. "The former waitress was able to confirm that there was once indeed a Harvey Girl at the Fray Marcos by the name of Clara in the nineteen-twenties and nineteen-thirties."

Although the name of the Grand Canyon Railway ghost has not been verified, it could very well be this former Harvey Girl now known only as "Clara." The ghost of Clara is simply a dedicated Harvey Girl who never forgot her customer-service skills, and simply missed the departure of the train to the afterlife.

BUCKY O'NEILL IS STILL ABOARD THE TRAIN

Riding to the Grand Canyon South Rim on the Grand Canyon Railway is an exciting experience for the young and old alike, especially on the extraordinary excursions when the old steam locomotives run. Long before there were Grand Canyon helicopter tours, air tours, whitewater rafting or even mule tours, there was the Grand Canyon's train. Before there were paved roads, Grand Canyon hotels, and even before the canyon was made into a national park, the Grand Canyon Railway brought curious travelers from all over the world to stand on the rim and gaze upon this wonder of the world.

I chatted with one of the Grand Canyon Railway engineers. Their group is made up of retired railroad men with a passion for old-style train travel.

"Do you believe the Grand Canyon Railway is haunted?" I asked the elderly engineer who proudly wore the uniform of his trade.

He sat down on a bench near the Grand Canyon Railway depot at the South Rim and motioned for me to join him.

"Well, they say it is," he smiled with a wink. "I haven't seen the ghost myself, but several of the train personnel and passengers say they have seen something."

"Really? Do they see the ghost along the rails? Or, has he been seen on the train?"

"The ghost looks like an old cowboy and he is often seen aboard the train." The engineer knew he had my interest now. "He rides in one of the cars as a passenger. Guests and staff see him sitting alone in a car one minute, and when they take a second look, they find that the man has disappeared."

"Do they know who the man might be?" I was awestruck.

"I believe it's none other than Bucky O'Neill." He had no doubt in his voice. "This railroad would not even be here if it wasn't for Bucky O'Neill. I think he comes along for the ride every once in a while to live out his dream."

Bucky O'Neill was born William Owen O'Neill in Missouri on February 2, 1860. He headed west and ended up in Arizona Territory in 1879. Prospecting led him to a copper deposit near Anita, fourteen miles south of Grand Canyon Village. Like many prospectors, he found mining not so profitable. He sold his land to the Santa Fe and Grand Canyon Railway Company. O'Neill recognized the potential for tourism, so he often spoke about the natural beauty of the canyon to anyone who would listen. He sought investments from the Santa Fe Railway for their support of his plan. He finally gained their trust and in 1897 the Santa Fe and Grand

Canyon Railway was incorporated. Tracks began to be laid between Williams and the South Rim.

O'Neill was known as an author, journalist, miner, lawman, judge and politician. He was also an American hero who lost his life as one of Teddy Roosevelt's Rough Riders fighting in the Spanish American War in 1898. Bucky O'Neill never lived to see his vision become a reality. He would have been proud to take that first rail ride between Williams and the Grand Canyon in September 1901.

One of the hostesses on the Grand Canyon Railway told me of an incident on one of the daily excursions to the Grand Canyon from Williams.

"It was on a weekend run and the train was full as usual," she said and handed me a bottle of water. "One of the passenger guests pulled me aside and commented on the realistic looking cowboy or reenactment player riding in the same car as his family. I knew the actors were all in a rear car getting ready to mingle with the passenger guests, so I smiled and asked which gentleman he was referring too."

The hostess waved to some of the morning passengers and continued her story.

"The passenger escorted me towards an empty seat in the car we were riding in. The man had a puzzled look on his face as we approached the unoccupied seat. He pointed to the vacant spot and his face went pale. We looked all around the car, but nobody could explain where the mysterious 'cowboy' disappeared to."

"Did you ever find him?" I asked.

"Well," she giggled, "on the way back from the Grand Canyon to Williams, the same passenger approached me again. He was carrying a book he had purchased at a Grand Canyon bookstore. He opened it to a certain page and showed me a picture of the cowboy he'd seen earlier that day on the train."

"Anyone we know?" I raised my eyebrows.

"It was Rough Rider Bucky O'Neill," she smiled. "Since then I've learned other passengers have seen him as well."

"Can't say I blame him," I chuckled. "This train ride will leave you spellbound!"

For information about the Grand Canyon Railway go to:
Grand Canyon Railway
1-800-843-8724; www.thetrain.com

WHITE GHOST OF KENDRICK PEAK

A mysterious snow-white deer has been seen by hunters throughout the Kaibab National Forest for over eighty years. "White Ghost," as the albino deer is known, is often seen south of the Grand Canyon off State Route 64. The buck was first sighted during the 1924 hunting season. A bounty of $500 was offered by a local taxidermist to whoever was lucky enough to bring in White Ghost's carcass. This was a considerable sum of money then, so the bounty fired up a lot of interest among local hunters. The reward money attracted professional deer hunters from all around the United States as well. No one could claim it.

The 1940 deer season brought a group of non-hunters to the area to look for White Ghost. They drove up and down the forest roads for days hoping for a glimpse of the elusive animal with the long whiskers. At last they spied the legendary deer through their binoculars. White Ghost seemed to be one step ahead of his predators. He knew ways to distance himself from the bounty hunters by scaling the steep mountain terrain. This amazed the athletic men, who thought they knew the rugged mountainside. They shook their heads and were baffled by White Ghost's agility. Very few mountain goats could descend the walls of stone, or leap off the edges of ravines into the brush below. This was not a challenge for White Ghost. One moment White Ghost was in a hunter's gunscope, and the next moment it was though he had vanished into thin air.

Some deer hunters have returned to the forest year after year for the chance of mounting the trophy of White Ghost on the wall of their den. It is not uncommon to see a pair of snow-white deer in the early morning hours. Soon, the huge white buck will appear alone—and just as quickly he will disappear silently. White Ghost is often spotted at night when its ashen coat shows up against the forest darkness in the "Land Where the Lion Screams." Although not marked on any Arizona map, this northern section of the state is rumored to be an area ripe with eerie tales of strange events.

One persistent hunter chased the deer for over two weeks. Every time the man came into shooting distance of the beast, White Ghost simply leaped off into another direction or descended deeper down into the woods and canyons. As the defeated gentleman walked off the mountain, White Ghost charged the man and nearly trampled him. The hunter swore White Ghost's gnashing teeth were laughing at him as it trotted back into the protective forest.

I spoke to an avid deer hunter named Charlie, who grew up in the area south of the Grand Canyon. I asked him if he had ever encountered or heard of the White Ghost.

"Yes, of course! I've heard the stories ever since I was a young boy," he chuckled. "I'd look for the White Ghost every time we went out during the hunting season. I think everyone up here has secretly pictured the White Ghost's rack of antlers hanging on the wall in their den."

"Do you know anyone who has seen the elusive deer?" I was curious.

"Well," Charlie hesitated, "I don't tell this story to many people, but I encountered 'White Ghost' when I was in my early twenties. I was hunting with an old high-school buddy. It was really cold that day. There was snow on the ground and it was hard to drive down the narrow forest roads."

Charlie paused to light a cigarette.

"We were ready to call it a day when I looked up and saw the ghostly deer on our left—just standing there near the ravine and staring us down. I raised my rifle to view him through the scope, but the deer had vanished. 'He's over here now!' my hunting buddy pointed to the mountain side on the right."

"How did the deer get over to the other side so fast?" I asked.

"I don't know," Charlie shook his head. "It was like a freaky illusion. One minute he was one side of the ravine, and the next minute he was halfway up the mountain on the other side of the ravine. He has to be a ghost—I don't see how there can be any other explanation."

Although seldom seen, White Ghost is revered by the locals, Grand Canyon tourists, and the deer hunters who are hesitant to shoot. After all, who really wants to destroy a legend?

HAUNTED
HULL
CABIN

A forest ranger by the name of J.D. Hunter told the *Williams* [Arizona] *News* about an encounter he had in the early 1980s with the ghost of John Hance. Hunter was working at the Hull Cabin Fire Guard Station, which is located in the Kaibab National Forest and one mile from the old Hance Trail.

J.D's two roommates had left for the evening to visit friends in Grand Canyon Village. He was looking forward to a quiet night alone at the isolated cabin. A thunderstorm began to brew in the distance, and flashes of lightning performed a dance across the darkening sky. The sun had been down for about an hour, but the light show almost made the barn and other objects on the property as visible as in daytime.

There was no electricity in the cabin when J.D. and his

fellow rangers resided at the historic site. Rangers used Coleman lanterns for night lighting. Hunter planned to clean his rifle that evening, and lit the mantle on the lantern. Alone, he could hear every creak and moan in the rustic log cabin.

Suddenly, he heard a noise on the front porch and then a knock on the door. He hadn't heard any vehicles pull up, and figured it was just some of his friends coming to visit unannounced.

"Come on in!" J.D. yelled and looked up at the door.

The door flung open hard just a as a roll of thunder cracked and a bolt of lightning flared across the sky much like what one sees in a horror movie. A gray-haired man in a worn overcoat stumbled into the cabin but stopped in the open door.

The older man told him he was looking for the "Hull boys." J.D. chuckled, thinking the old man was simply a joking tourist.

"No..." Hunter was puzzled, "the 'Hull boys' aren't here."

"Didn't think so," the old man scratched his gray whiskers. Brothers Philip and William Hull came to the Grand Canyon in the early 1880s with a herd of sheep and a part-time employee—and hopeful prospector—by the name of John Hance.

John Hance arrived at the South Rim of the Grand Canyon around 1883 and is reputedly the canyon's first non–Native American resident. He built a cabin east of Grandview Point at the trailhead of an ancient Indian trail he improved to allow access to his asbestos mining claim in the canyon. The trail, known as the Old Hance Trail by historians, soon became Grand Canyon's first tourist trail. Hance quickly realized there was more money to be made taking wide-eyed tourists deep into the canyon, than there was in asbestos mining.

Hance delighted in telling canyon stories to the visitors—most of them tall tales rather than mere facts. With a straight face, Hance told guests how he had dug the canyon himself, piling the excavated earth down near Flagstaff—a dirt pile now known as the San Francisco Peaks. Hance left a lasting legacy at the Grand Canyon, passing away in 1919, the year the Grand Canyon became a national park. Hance was the first person buried in what would become the Grand Canyon Pioneer Cemetery.

Ranger Hunter invited the man to stay and wait out the rainstorm. He thought it was the neighborly thing to do, and it would give him some company on such an eerie evening. The old man nodded and shut the cabin door. J.D. introduced himself and offered his handshake.

"I'm John," the old man said looking around the cabin "Most people call me Captain." J.D. offered John a beer but the old man declined. He removed a bottle from his overcoat and plopped it down on the wooden table. "Brought my own."

He removed his overcoat and hung it over the back of the chair. He slowly sat down in the chair and scooted in closer to the table. His blue-gray eyes looked weary in the lantern light. J.D recognized the man to be the legendary Captain John Hance—he was sure of it.

Hance told the younger man that he lived not too far from there. He shook his head and removed the cork from the bottle of brownish amber brew. He tipped back the bottle and swallowed a few sips of the drink.

He told J.D. he noticed the barn door was locked. Hance wanted to know if he could keep his mule dry in the barn during the storm. J.D. handed him the key. "Help yourself. Wish there was some feed out there for your animal, but there isn't."

Hance stood up slowly and headed for the door. J.D., dumbfounded, sat at the table wondering if the phantom would return. Indeed, Hance returned, dripping wet, about fifteen minutes later. The captain pulled out a blood-soaked burlap bag from under his overcoat. It was full of squirrels.

Hance grinned and boasted of having good luck hunting earlier that day. The squirrels were already cleaned and ready to cook. J.D. heated up the stove as the old man began to build a fire in the fireplace. He talked about having spent the night with the Hulls, there in the cabin, on several occasions. Soon, the squirrels were sizzling in a large frying pan.

J.D. asked Hance how many routes, rim to rim, he had done in the Grand Canyon. Without any hesitation he answered eleven. He crossed his arms and went deep into thought. "Hopi Salt, Seth's Trail, Red Canyon, Berry's Trail," he counted on his fingers. "Cameron Trail, Rust Route, Louis Trail, Bass rim to rim, Topocoba, Prospect, and Diamond Creek."

"Have you ever been on Apollo Temple?" J.D. asked.

"Yeh," nodded the ghost of John Hance. "Who do you think put the cairns on top of it?"

J.D removed the frying pan from the stove and glanced at the table. The old man's ghost had vanished!

Guests can rent Hull Cabin for overnight stays.
For information, contact:
Kaibab National Forest
Tusayan Ranger Station
PO Box 3088
Grand Canyon, AZ 86023
918-638-2443

THE TERROR
OF THE
DEATH TRAP

The Hualapai are a Native American tribe in Mohave County near the west end of the Grand Canyon. The tribe is said to have known about the "Death Trap"—a rock that kills, from prehistoric days.

A book called *Lost Mines and Hidden Treasure* (1971) by Leland Lovelace explains that the Death Trap is in a narrow gorge, a little pass in a rugged, almost inaccessible mountain in the Cerbat Range. The locale has been of great interest to hunters and prospectors, for this mountain is a hideaway of antelope and bighorn sheep. It also lies in gold and silver country. In fact, it was a group of hunters who were credited with the first non–Native American report of the Death Trap.

Around 1883, a group of men building the Santa Fe Railway across Arizona took a weekend off to go hunting in the Cerbats. From their base camp, the hunters witnessed a bright, steady light on the mountainside. They were intrigued by the glowing light, and decided to make a few inquiries of the locals. Some of the Hualapais told them about the "power in the rock," but refused to go into any further details of the legend.

The Death Trap story came into focus again in 1895. A group of hunters frightened a bighorn sheep in the Cerbats, and it ran frantically into the narrow gorge beneath the overhanging ledge. The hunters stood still and observed the sheep with awe. They never fired a shot, but watched in terror as the bighorn fell dead upon the rock. After witnessing the animal's eerie death, the hunters slowly approached to investigate. Suddenly, out of nowhere, a ghostly spirit of an old Hualapai Indian jumped out of the brush and completely startled them. With hand signals and animated words, he tried to ward the hunters off.

He told them the sheep had stepped upon the Death Trap and if they followed after it, they would die just as the unfortunate sheep had. He pointed to many sun-bleached bones that had fallen from the rock down into the gorge.

The hunters stood staring at the rock not knowing what to do. A rattlesnake crawled out of the crevice and slithered to the edge of the blue rock. It coiled, raised its head, and fell dead as a door knob. The bewildered hunters looked at each other in disbelief. They thanked the elder for saving their lives and watched him vanish in front of them.

The Hualapai elders tell this story: Long ago a mysterious stranger came to the Hualapais seeking food and shelter. The man had golden blond hair, intense blue eyes, and a handsome face—but he was severely hunchbacked. His body was small, shrunken and grotesquely deformed. The little troll-like person had strange powers for healing the sick and injured, sometimes by just focusing his large blue eyes upon the ailing patient. Animals loved him and seemed to follow him everywhere.

The chief of the tribe trusted the stranger beyond words. He made the outsider the tribal medicine man. After a while, the tribe noticed that time had no aging effect upon him. Others grew old and feeble, the children matured, but the blond, blue-eyed hunchback never seemed to change.

One day the hunchback's luck drastically changed when he violated the chief's trust. The son of the chief was soon to marry a beautiful young woman. Just before the ceremonies were to begin, the bride disappeared. Everyone was bewildered and couldn't figure out what had happened. Then, an elderly woman confided to the chief that she had seen the blue-eyed medicine man use his magic to whisk the bride away.

Everyone loved the hunchbacked man so much that, rather than kill him, they decided to exile him from the village. After giving him a head start, a dozen of the tribesmen were sent to pursue him to be sure he kept on going, but then an eerier thing happened.

The tribesmen gradually realized that they were now following the mysterious man, not chasing. He was leading them on, and as if drawn by some magnetic field, they could not stop or retrace their steps. When the chief sent other runners to bring the warriors back, they did not listen to the commands. They continued to follow the former medicine man without stopping to rest.

Things became even stranger. The runners chasing the first group of tribesmen became suddenly spellbound. They saw the dozen braves fall, one by one, dead in their tracks as soon as they stepped onto the parted segments of an enormous blue stone.

The Hualapais say the strange blond medicine man invoked into the stone the fateful power of the gods to end the chase of the stolen Hualapai bride and himself.

Some geologists believe that maybe this rock is a highly radioactive chunk of uranium. Uranium and other rare minerals have been found in the mountains of Mohave County and elsewhere in northern Arizona, but it is not known if a chunk of uranium could be so "hot" in its radioactivity that it could kill an animal on contact.

While some Hualapai tribesmen have mixed feelings about whether the story is true, some local historians have their own theory. Traditionally, when a Hualapai leader died, they cremated that person and destroyed his worldly goods. It is possible they considered the leader's horses and livestock as part of his worldly goods, had them killed, and that may be why animal bones were piled up here and there.

The Death Trap may have simply been a Hualapai legend to keep others away from their burial grounds. Nevertheless, I do not suggest touching the glowing blue stone at any cost. The ghosts of the tribesmen who chased the hunchback and died doing so could take revenge.

PAIUTE GHOST DANCERS

One of the favorite songs of the Paiute Ghost Dancers includes this refrain:

> *The snow lies there—ro-rani!*
> *The snow lies there—ro-rani!*
> *The snow lies there—ro-rani!*
> *The snow lies there—ro-rani!*
> *The Milky Way lies there.*
> *The Milky Way lies there.*

The Ghost Dance is held in the open air at night. Stars shine down on the wide extending plain, which is ringed by tall mountains, a fringe of dark pine trees at their base and their peaks tipped white with snow.

In this setting, the song of the mountain snow and the stars of the Milky Way—road of the dead to the spirit world

—stretching across the clear sky, evokes in the Paiute a feeling of home-love.

Their ancestors conducted the Ghost Dance ceremony in isolated places where the side canyon of Kanab Creek begins to form an outer edge to the Grand Canyon.

Jack Wilson, a Paiute spiritual leader formerly known as Wovoka, was believed to have had a vision during the solar eclipse on January 1, 1889. A gifted young leader, he preached the message of universal love. He often presided over circle dances that symbolized the sun's heavenly path across the sky.

Wilson received a message that his tribe must love each other, not fight, and live in peace with the white man. The people must work, not steal or lie, and they must not engage in war or self-mutilation practices connected with mourning the dead. If they would abide by these rules, they would be united with friends and family in the "other world."

In God's presence, there would be no sickness, disease, or old age. Wilson was given the Ghost Dance and instructed to take it to his people. If the dance was performed properly, the performers could secure their happiness, and they could cross over between the living and the dead. Whites would leave the land, and dead ancestors and vanished wild game would return to enjoy a life of abundance.

During the ceremony they made white paintings on the sandstone cliffs near the largest known source of white pigment. It is not known if the paintings were a part of the ritual or a way of recording the ceremony.

Both traditional and nontraditional vision-seeking methods were used to enter a trance state during the early Ghost Dance movements. Some dancers would go into trances and experience visits by ghosts of their ancestors. The dance often transfixed participants as they connected with the dead in another plane. Some dancers would pass out and fall to the ground looking dead—like a ghost.

One traditional method was to visit one of the rock art locations to fast and pray for a dream. Sometimes answers came through the dancing and rituals associated with the ceremony. Families have brought their children there for decades to learn the customs and messages of the Ghost Dance which are carefully painted on the stone canyon walls.

The Paiute and Hualapai dancers say the Ghost Dance ceremony lasted five days and nights. They danced each night and, on the last evening, the dancing continued until morning. Trances and movements became part of the ceremony, which was repeated every six weeks. Soon the religion spread from the Paiute to many other western Native American tribes, each of whom adapted it to their own traditions. The Sioux, for example, created white garments called "ghost shirts" that they believed would provide protection from evil and the soldiers' bullets.

The Kanab Creek Canyon wilderness area is said to be very spiritual and magical to visitors. To reach the western side of Kanab Creek Wilderness, take the Mt. Trumbull Road (Mohave County Road 109) south from SR 389 to Hacks Canyon Road (BLM 1023—open to high-clearance four-wheel-drive vehicles only). The eastern side can be reached via Forest Roads 22, 201, 233 and 423 off US 89A. The easiest way to find your way around: get a copy of the Arizona Strip District Visitor Map.

GRAND CANYON CAVERNS AND WALTER PECK'S GHOST

The Caverns Inn and nearby Grand Canyon Caverns have been a stopping point for rafters and hikers of the Havasu Canyon Trail for many years. For some of these explorers, it's the first sign of civilization, where they can get an icy cold drink, hot meal, or a shower.

Grand Canyon Caverns is a separate operation from Grand Canyon National Park and is not connected with the National Park Service. But since it is another gateway to Colorado River rafting and the last pit stop for hikers to the Havasu hilltop, its ghost tale is well worth including.

In 1927, a young cowboy woodcutter by the name of Walter Peck was heading to his weekly poker game at a nearby railroad siding yard. As he followed the well traveled trail, he nearly plummeted into a large funnel shaped hole. Startled, he continued on to the card game. Peck couldn't wait to tell his friends about the mysterious gaping hole he almost tumbled in to. His tale sparked some interest in the other cowboys, so they planned to explore the site at sunrise.

Equipped with ropes and lanterns, Peck, his brother Miles, and the cowboys congregated around the ominous opening. One of the members of the impromptu expedition was secured with a rope harness and lowered down into the depths of the dark hole. Once the explorer reached the bottom, he lit a lantern and began to explore the area around him. The light shown on what he thought was a glistening vein of gold. He filled his pockets and a small bag with samples, and tugged on the rope to be lifted 150 feet back out of the cave.

He poured the samples out on the ground as he described things he saw in the wondrous cave. He told his partners of seeing two human skeletons and the remains of a horse saddle about fifty feet down into the shaft. Peck purchased the land and caverns immediately. His friends were ecstatic over their grand discovery and dreamed of being rich. But, when the assay report came back, the gold nuggets were merely iron oxide, or rust.

This did stop the enterprising Walter. Since he already owned the land, he came up with a new idea to make his investment worthwhile. Peck decided to charge a twenty-five-cent fee for any brave adventurer who wished to see the skeletons—which he advertised as the remains of prehistoric cavemen. Guests were guided down into the cave by means of a primitive elevator where they were secured with rope and lowered down by a hand-cranked winch.

The Civilian Conservation Corps built a new entrance into the cave in 1935. A wooden staircase, three ladders, and a sixty-foot swinging bridge were the only means of access into the caverns until 1962. It was then that a modern elevator was installed, and the natural entrance of the cave was sealed.

To draw motorists to the new discovery, a 1927 advertisement read: "Preserved bodies of ancient Stone Age Cavemen found in their lair in the high desert of Arizona. Fabulous gold strike only a mile from US 66—the Main Street of America."

The Hualapai Indians explained the discovery of the human remains. In 1917-1918, the years of the deadly Spanish flu epidemic, two of the tribesmen had taken ill with the disease while gathering wood, and perished. The ground was frozen so their bodies were lowered into the pit. The broken horse saddle was placed near the dead to provide their spirits a final ride across the Great Divide. The old cavern entrance is known as a Native American sacred burial site, and the caverns were considered a holy place. Perhaps the spirits of these tribesmen still wander their cavernous tomb.

In the 1950s, the skeletal remains of an extinct Harlan's ground sloth, *Glossotherium harlani*, were also found in the cave. The giant sloth was moved to the University of Arizona in Tucson in 1961. The sloth, nicknamed "Gertie," apparently fell into the cave, and was found where it had died—trying to claw its way to freedom. The beast has been extinct for at least 20,000 years, measured fifteen feet long and weighed about one ton. A mummified bobcat that fell into the cavern a century ago was found in the spot where he broke his hip.

Hauntingly, stacked in the center of the cavern are U.S. government survival rations to feed two thousand refugees for two weeks. These barrels of rations have been in place in the cave since the 1962 Cuban missile crisis. Ironically, they provided only three rolls of toilet paper for the throng of survivors. Now that's scary!

In 1958, it was discovered that the cavern's Mystery Room seemed to have an airshaft that reached into the Grand Canyon. People experimented by pumping red smoke into one of the cave holes. Weeks later, and forty miles away, that smoke began to flow down into the Grand Canyon near Havasu Falls.

Workers in the caverns have ghost stories too. They believe the restaurant, curio shop and the caverns are all haunted by Walter Peck. The office manager said that sometimes when she is working in the office, she hears the elevator going up and down into the caverns even though the center is closed and the elevator is supposed to be turned off. Light fixtures have been seen shaking or swinging back and forth at odd hours of the day and night when the place is empty.

Another employee also confirmed she has heard the elevator running up and down the shaft after it had been turned off for the night. She has witnessed the elevator and caverns lights turning on and off on their own as well. The staff member has heard the sounds of the tables and chairs being moved around in the restaurant after closing. When she returned to the dining room to check out the disturbance, she found everything placed in its proper position. She has also heard "radio static–like" conversations by unseen guests in the dining hall.

Grand Canyon Caverns now offer visitors a chance to sleep with the ghosts deep into the cave. You take the elevator down 22 stories underground and spend the night on a furnished motel room platform in a place so quiet and dark, so large and so old, and so alone, except for the shadowy spirits that still roam the pathways.

Some guests visiting the caverns have felt an unseen presence near them as they were taking one of the guided tours. Sometimes they see a guest not originally on their tour appear in the group—and then suddenly, the ghostly guest is no longer a part of the excursion. At times there seems to be an extra person riding in the elevator. One minute the mystery rider is there, and the next second they have disappeared. Most guests just laugh it off and say it is Walter Peck and his poker buddies playing practical jokes on cave visitors!

Grand Cavern Canyons
P.O. Box 180, Rt 66
Peach Springs, AZ 86434
928-422-4565; www.grandcanyoncaverns.com

GHOSTS OF MOONEY FALLS

everal Native American tribes live on the plateau above the Grand Canyon, but the Havasupai are the only ones who make their homes *in* the canyon. Their name means "people of the blue-green water," which may come from the color of Havasu Creek. They belong to one of the smallest and most isolated tribes in the country, and live in a side chasm called Havasu near the bottom of the Grand Canyon. The only way to reach the Havasupai Village is by horseback or hiking eight miles into the depths of the Havasu Canyon. Although helicopters do fly in and out of the secluded village, mail and supplies are still carried in by pack horses each day.

The Havasupai people say that, long ago, the walls of the canyon regularly closed together, killing anyone who ventured into it. An elderly woman who lived up at the top had two very handsome sons. They wanted to hunt the deer and antelope that roamed the land, but they did not have the materials to make arrows. Their wise mother warned them against wandering into the canyon to gather the strong reeds that grew there, but the young men were foolish and full of adventure. They chopped down two juniper logs and trekked down into the deep canyon, balancing the huge logs on top of their heads. Soon, the canyon walls began to rumble as they closed in on the young men. They acted quickly, and placed the juniper logs between the moving canyon walls. The logs held the walls apart so that the men could gather the reeds for constructing their arrows.

To the Havasupai, Havasu Falls is the key to the beginning of all mankind. They believe that when two gods were at war with each other, the evil god drowned the entire universe. Only one person survived the great flood—the daughter of the kind and compassionate god. She had hid in a log that floated in the waters for many days until it came to rest on top of Humphrey's Peak. Crawling out of the log, she found herself all alone. She wandered endlessly without companionship and was very afraid. One morning she lay down and opened herself up to the rays of the sun and conceived a son. As time went on she began to yearn for another child. She wandered into the Havasu Canyon where she encountered the beautiful waterfalls. Here with the waterfall she conceived a daughter. The two children grew, married, and gave birth to all humanity.

The hike to Havasu Canyon is considered moderately difficult. It starts off steep and winds down switchbacks for one and a half miles. The trail is rugged and rocky. But, as anyone will tell you, this is one of the most beautiful hikes into the Grand Canyon. The anticipation of viewing the majestic Havasu Falls and climbing down the rugged terrain to the pools of Mooney Falls—one mile farther down the trail—overrides the pain of the ten-mile hike to the campgrounds.

As you near Havasupai Village you will notice two natural irregular red pillars carved by the elements. They seem to be about ten feet in diameter and forty feet high. They are called the Wigeleeva, and some say they are a god and a goddess. Other tribal members say they represent the petrified remains of two brothers, tribal chiefs of long ago, who led that Indians into Havansu Canyon and are still standing guard over them. Some of the older tribesmen say that when the Wigeleeva fall down, the world will end.

Mooney Falls is the tallest of the four major waterfalls in Havasu Canyon. Standing near the 198-foot drop, one can imagine what an Irishman, Daniel W. Mooney, must have felt when he first glanced down at the travertine-encrusted waterfall. Travertine is a form of limestone that occurs near hot bubbling mineral springs. An object—such as a corpse—lying on the rocks would become permanently encased as the travertine accumulates and dries around it.

The Havasupai people have their own name for this magnificent waterfall, but they do not share it with the scores of adventurers who come down into their canyon. On our maps the roaring waterfall is named for Mooney, the Irish sailor and prospector who came into the canyon looking for gold in 1880.

Mooney wanted to descend the cliff near the falls, so he asked his companions to lower him over the side with a 150-foot rope. The rope was 50 feet too short, and left Mooney dangling beside the waterfall. Because of the roaring torrent, his men didn't hear his calls to be pulled back up—nor could he climb the rope to the top. Some historians speculate his partners severed the rope, but most likely it simply frayed on the rough edges of the travertine rock.

The helpless man swayed back and forth on the unraveling rope until he plunged to his death in the blue green pool of water below. His colleagues hiked out of the canyon and did not return until several months later. When they blasted out a tunnel that took them down to the pool, they found Mooney's body—hauntingly encased in travertine. They buried him near the bottom of the falls. Daniel Mooney's ghost, the Havasupai say, is still digging and hammering, his spirit continuing to mine in the caves below the waterfall.

There is a canyon near Mooney Falls where many of the dead Havasupai were cremated in the earlier times—hence its name of Ghost Canyon. According to the Havasupai belief, when a person dies, their ghost lingers near their possessions. Anyone who touches them could be carried off by the ghost to be his companion in death. Because of this, no one treasures possessions of the deceased—but rather shuns them.

Following a Havasupai's death today, his house is abandoned for many weeks. In olden times it was burned down. If the dead man owned fruit trees, these days one or two may be cut down. In the past, all the trees might have been cut, and his crops destroyed.

The deceased's coffin is placed in a large wooden crate. Mourners place items that belonged to the dead atop the coffin and into the crate, along with things of their own they wish to give as propitiatory presents. They might add the saddle or boots belonging to the deceased. There would be food, clothing, money and blankets placed in the crate. Then the crate is nailed shut. Most of the dead are buried in out-of-the-way corners of the canyon; the main burial ground is near the waterfalls below the village. There are no grave markers. Visitors to the campground are rarely aware they are within a few yards of a cemetery and the ancient ghosts of Havasupai Canyon.

Hikers experience a wide variety of emotions while hiking the canyon. Some say it is awe-inspiring, while others become more sensitive to everything around them. Hiker Adam Holschuh told me of his hiking experience to Havasu Canyon.

"In 2006, three friends and I hiked down into Havasupai Falls. On the second day, we went exploring down the river from our campsite, and found a cave about a mile away [from] Mooney Falls. We hiked down into the cave, and noticed some sketches on the wall which were either scratched with stones, or chalk. They looked like hieroglyphics, but not the Egyptian kind —it was like nothing I've ever seen before. There was also a circle drawn on the floor and I noticed some blood stains in the middle. It was pretty creepy, so we left the cave.

"Outside of the cave, my friend noticed a huge stone that was in the shape of a throne. I couldn't believe how perfectly shaped it was. My friend wanted to get a picture sitting in it, so he gave me his camera to take the photograph. I snapped the picture, but when I went to hand the camera back to him, it fell. The dirt in the area was so fine from erosion— some of it seeped into the camera and ruined it completely. From there, things on the trip went downhill fast.

"That night after we went to bed, my friend Rex heard something walking around in our campground. He climbed out of his tent to investigate, but didn't see anyone. Then, he thought he heard footsteps walking off into the forest. He tried to follow them, got lost, and fell in the river. Luckily the same noise woke me up, and I was there just in time to pull him out as he floated by the campsite.

"The next day there was a terrible flash flood which caused the water level in the falls and the river to rise dramatically. We almost drowned trying to get back to our campsite to move to higher ground. After the flood, we decided that we had enough. We packed up and headed back to Phoenix. When I returned home, I found out that my stepdad (who was like a real father to me) had passed away unexpectedly. The trip seemed to be a complete disaster."

Holschuh added even more mystery to his story. The following year, they decided to go back to Havasu Canyon, believing everything would be better. To make a long story short, it flooded again. They heard the footsteps as before, waking them up at least once every night. And sadly, his friend Rex's dad died while they were down in the canyon. He could chalk the nightly footsteps up to an overactive imagination, but the fact that it flooded really badly each time they were there, and that both of their dads died on different trips really made him wonder if that cave and/or throne did not have some type of curse attached to it.

The spirits could have been warning the young men of the tragedies awaiting them in Phoenix, hastening them to pack up and go home where they were needed. Perhaps the footsteps in the forest were their fathers coming to say goodbye. Havasu Canyon has a mystical feel to it, and definitely a veil to the other world.

If you go: Havasupai Tourism manages and operates tourism activities including guided and unguided tours, a 200-person campground near Havasu Falls, and a horse packing business in which tribal members serve as guides and provide saddle and pack horses that carry goods and visitors in and out of the canyon.

The Tribal Packers Enterprise accepts reservations from tourists, and schedules various tribe members as providers. Please contact:
P.O. Box 160
Supai, AZ 86435
1-928-448-2121
1-928-448-2141
1-928-448-2174
1-928-448-2180
http://www.havasupaitribe.com

Suran, William C.
The Kolb Brothers of the Grand Canyon 1991

Evans, Edna
Tales from the Grand Canyon 1985

Stampoulos, Linda L.
Images of America: Visiting the Grand Canyon 2004

Thybony, Scott
Incredible Grand Canyon: Cliffhangers and Curiosities 2007

Grattan, Virginia, L
Mary Colter: Builder Upon the Red Earth 1980

Berke, Arnold
Mary Colter: Architect of the Southwest 2002

Henry, Margurite
Brighty of the Grand Canyon 1953

Poling-Kempes, Leslie
The Harvey Girls: Women who Opened the West 1991

Lago, Don
Grand Canyon Trivia 2009

DeMente, Boye Lafayette
Grand Canyon Answer Book 1989

Berger, Todd R.
It Happened at Grand Canyon 2007

Hunter, J. D.
Williams News 1980

ABOUT THE AUTHOR

Debe Branning has been the director of the MVD Ghost-chasers of Mesa/Bisbee paranormal team since 1995. The team conducts investigations of haunted, historical locations throughout Arizona. For the past ten years she has led Spirit Workshops that provides ghost hunters, paranormal team members, and folks wanting to try the art of ghost hunting a chance to work and learn techniques together. Debe has been a guest lecturer at Ottawa University, Central Arizona College, Arizona State University and South Mountain Community College. She has been a speaker at SciFi Conventions such as CopperCon, FiestaCon, HauntedCon and AZParaCon. She appeared in an episode of Travel Channel's "Ghost Stories" about haunted Jerome, Arizona, in 2010. Debe is the author of *Sleeping with Ghosts: A Ghost Hunter's Guide to Arizona's Haunted Hotels and Inns* and two children's books. She pens a column for Examiner.com titled "Arizona Haunted Sites" so that travelers will know where they might find a ghost or two when they visit Arizona.

A native of Omaha, Nebraska, Debe has resided in Mesa, Arizona, for over thirty years. During this time, she has traveled to every corner of the state studying Arizona's history and culture, and enjoying haunted places along the way.

Contact Debe Branning at: www.mvdghostchasers.com, or www.examiner.com/x-2345-Arizona-Haunted-Sites-Examiner.

Q. Where can you get answers to hundreds of questions about your favorite national parks?
A. In the National Parks Trivia Series!

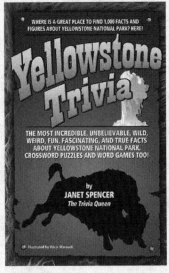